Mary Berry's
Stress-free Kitchen

Mary Berry's
Stress-free Kitchen

120 New and Updated Recipes for Easy Entertaining

headline

For Annabel and Tom and their families who bring great joy and sunshine to our lives

Some of the recipes in the book have previously appeared in
Mary Berry's New Aga Cookbook, *Cook Now, Eat Later* and *Real Food – Fast*

First published in 2008 by HEADLINE PUBLISHING GROUP
First published in softback in 2010 by HEADLINE PUBLISHING GROUP

1

Cataloguing in Publication Data is available from the British Library
ISBN 978 0 7553 1730 1

Set in Segoe by Fiona Pike

Photographs on pages 40, 45, 56, 138, 141, 144, 158, 160, 182, 193, 194 by Peter Cassidy
Photographs on pages 18, 25, 36, 46, 68, 88, 102, 148, 170, 178, 189 by James Murphy
Photographs on pages 23, 27, 51, 59, 108, 137, 147, 157, 163, 190 by Juliet Piddington
Photographs on pages 4, 11, 93, 96, 119, 174 by William Shaw
Designed by Fiona Pike
Edited by Susan Fleming
Printed and bound by Imago

Headline's policy to use papers that are natural, renewable and recyclable products and made from wood grown in sustainable forests. The logging and manufacturing processes are expected to conform to the environmental regulations of the country of origin.

HEADLINE PUBLISHING GROUP
An Hachette UK Company
338 Euston Road
London NW1 3BH

www.headline.co.uk
www.hachette.co.uk

Contents

Acknowledgements

My thanks are due as always to the special few who have worked with me on this book.

At home, my assistant Lucy Young, who has been with me now for nineteen years, has masterminded every detail and kept us all on track. Lucinda Kaizik helped us with the testing of the recipes and is our memory when we get distracted! All three of us have the same goal: to make foolproof recipes that taste delicious and have the wow factor. My husband Paul and my children (and grandchildren) are sterling tasters.

At Headline, I owe huge thanks to two friends who have worked with me over many years and many books – Celia Kent and Susan Fleming. What fun we have had with such a happy team. Celia Levett was also very helpful, as were Jo Roberts-Miller and Lorraine Jerram.

But the biggest debt is to you, the readers who buy my books. Because of you, I have to keep up to the mark, and I am enabled to carry on doing something that I love – cooking.

Introduction

In a sense, my kitchen has been stress-free throughout almost my entire married life. For a start, because I love cooking, trying out new recipes or ingredients has never caused me a moment's worry. In fact, it gives me great pleasure. But I admit I have always been a reasonably organised cook, and I think the key to a stress-free kitchen is based on several elements: good planning in advance, careful shopping, a sensible store-cupboard, using simple cooking techniques, and doing as much preparation and cooking beforehand as possible – which usually involves the freezer. It all boils down ultimately to good organisation.

If that sounds too dictatorial, it's not meant to be. For instance, it won't take you long to check the store-cupboard and fridge to see what is missing or running low. Make a list, too, of things needed for the week's family meals. Have you run out of risotto rice? Is there enough milk in the fridge, and a back-up in the freezer, or should you buy more? Once you have decided what you will cook, make a similar list when you are giving a lunch or dinner party. That's forward planning.

With your menus for the week organised, then you can shop more cannily. Buy fresh foods from your good local butcher, fishmonger, greengrocer and baker, or – if you are lucky enough – from your local farmers' market. You can order special things well in advance – that beef fillet, or those prawns: another thing taken care of. You can get some ready-made ingredients from your corner shop or supermarket. I'm thinking about store-cupboard items like canned chopped tomatoes, tomato passata, jars of olives, creamed horseradish, cooked peppers or mayonnaise. I don't think one should feel guilty about buying these sorts of ingredients, they can transform dishes with flavour and texture and they're definitely not cheating. Many of these things are delicious in themselves, and using them will save you time, energy and stress. For instance, I could not survive without stock cubes, and they have come to my rescue on more than one occasion. Once, I had enough soup to feed four (half a pint per head), and an extra mouth turned up. All I had to do was make up the extra half-pint with a cube and some milk or water.

Keeping your store-cupboard well stocked is another element of the stress-free kitchen. You want to have in it, though, the things you most often use, so that you don't have to make a panicked dash to the shops at the last minute. And do you really need those jars or cans that have been lurking at the back of the shelves for years, knowing full well that you'll never use them? Recently, I've decided to rationalise the contents of my store-cupboard, and now I buy only dark soy sauce, medium curry powder and green pesto, for instance, which means I won't be attracted to any new alternatives I might not like. That's already taken a certain amount of stress out of buying, and gives me an inherent confidence when about to embark on a recipe or a meal.

After stress-free planning and shopping comes cooking. My cooking has always been fairly simple, relying on the most basic of techniques – with an occasional foray into something a little more fancy. I cook this way because I feel that good basic ingredients need nothing too complicated done to them to make them taste good. Thus all the recipes in this book are infinitely do-able, with no elaborate sauces, out-of-the-ordinary techniques, or ingredients that you might have to search out from the Hungarian deli in the next town! I hope that when you embark on any one of the recipes here that all potential stress will evaporate, as soon as you see how basically simple they are.

A major feature of many of my books in the past has been pre-preparing and pre-cooking, and this must be one of the best ways in which to keep stress out of the kitchen. If you have prepared a cold starter and pudding before a supper party, at least a day in advance (often much earlier), then your worries will be fewer on the day itself. If you have planned, shopped for, pre-cooked and frozen a Coq au Vin for lunch the Sunday after next (and it should be well labelled), then everything else will be virtually plain sailing.

Never forget that the freezer is an extremely valuable tool of the stress-free kitchen: in it you can store whole made-up dishes, garnishes (like croûtons), leftovers (to turn into something else delicious), stocks (for soups and sauces), and gluts of fruit and veg from the garden. Knowing there is a small container of frozen raspberries there ready to be whizzed into a coulis gives me confidence that I have something to tart up plain vanilla ice cream at a moment's notice. I use my freezer as a bank, making occasional valuable withdrawals, but also depositing gems every now and then (those split almonds that I can never find in the shops when I need them).

To my mind, organisation alleviates potential stress in the kitchen, and I hope that my ideas will help you take the heat out of your cooking.

Mary Berry

Canapés

As readers of my books will know well, I greatly enjoy giving parties. Sometimes when I have invited people over for a dinner party, I will give them canapés – little and varied bites to eat – which serve as a first course before we actually sit down at the table. And when I am having a drinks-only party – usually over holiday weekends, at Christmas or New Year – I like to offer a selection of canapés as well. Traditionally canapés are fiddly to prepare, and take up a lot of time on the day of a party, which can cause stress. The recipes here aren't difficult, however, and most of them can be made well in advance (often weeks in advance and frozen). All you have to do on the day is at most a gentle reheat and an attractive arrangement on a platter.

And never forget about the things that come ready-made, such as good olives – stoned and/or perhaps stuffed with feta, those delicious vegetable crisps, and savoury nuts. You could buy some dips, and offer a selection of prepared vegetables, breadsticks or mini pittas to dip into them. Smoked salmon can be rolled into little tubes (perhaps around some interesting filling), and that wouldn't take any time at all. There are many such possibilities to consider, which are quick, easy and stress-free – although I do like to offer something home-made as well.

Red House Blues

The name came about because I was introduced to the recipe by our dear friend Joan Heath, who lives in The Red House. This is my version of her delicious biscuits, which can be made ahead and baked as and when you need them. Remember to reduce the cooking time slightly for the smaller biscuits.

75g (3 oz) shelled walnuts
75g (3 oz) Stilton cheese, or any leftover blue cheese, grated
1 teaspoon English mustard powder
150g (5 oz) plain flour

100g (4 oz) butter, at room temperature
salt and freshly ground black pepper
50g (2oz) Parmesan, coarsely grated

Preheat the oven to 180°C/Fan 160°C/Gas 4.

1 Process the walnuts very briefly until roughly chopped, then tip out of the processor. Put the rest of the ingredients into the processor, saving one-third of the Parmesan for the topping, and process until the mixture is just beginning to form a ball. Add the chopped walnuts and process again for 2–3 seconds.

2 Turn on to a floured surface, divide the mixture in two and roll out each to form an even sausage shape about 15cm (6 in) long. (NB if you are using these as an accompaniment for cheese, make the sausage about 6cm/2½ in in diameter. If using as biscuits to have with drinks, divide the mixture again and make into even smaller rolls.) Wrap in clingfilm and chill or freeze, until the biscuit roll is really firm.

3 Slice the sausages into discs about 5mm (¼ in) thick, and spread out on two baking sheets greased or lined with non–stick paper. Sprinkle each biscuit with the reserved Parmesan.

4 Bake in the preheated oven for about 15–20 minutes, or until pale golden at the edges.

5 Remove from the oven and cool on a cooling rack.

Makes about 30–40, according to size

TO PREPARE AHEAD
Complete to the end of step 2 and keep chilled for 2–3 days. Freezes well raw or cooked for up to 2 months. If cooked refresh in a low oven until crisp.

TO COOK IN THE AGA
2-oven Aga: Bake on the grid shelf on the floor of the Roasting Oven with the cold plain shelf on the second set of runners, for about 10–15 minutes, watching carefully until pale golden at the edges.

3- or 4-oven Aga: Bake on the grid shelf on the floor of the Baking Oven for 10–15 minutes, watching carefully. If getting too brown, slide the cold plain shelf on to the second set of runners.

After thawing from frozen, crisp up in the Simmering Oven for about 30 minutes before serving.

Parma Ham, Goat's Cheese and Rocket Canapés

These are perfect cold canapés, delicious and quick to make. Although they are best made on the day, you can prepare them up to 10 hours ahead and keep in the fridge. Dill pickle cucumbers, sold in jars, are a sweeter version of gherkins and look exactly like large gherkins, but I much prefer them for flavour.

8 slices Parma ham
 1 x 150g tub of Chavroux or
  other soft goat's cheese
salt and freshly ground black
  pepper

2 large dill pickle cucumbers
1 x 70g bag rocket

1 Lay each piece of Parma ham on a board, and cut off and discard any surplus fat. Spread 1 good teaspoon of goat's cheese over the end quarter. Season lightly.

2 Slice each pickled cucumber thinly lengthways into 4. Lay 1 slice of cucumber over the goat's cheese. Take a small handful of rocket and lay on top, leaving some of the rocket sticking out at the ends.

3 Roll the Parma ham into a cigar shape and transfer to the fridge until needed.

4 Slice each roll in half and arrange, standing up on the cut side, on a serving platter. Serve cold.

Makes 16

TO PREPARE AHEAD
These can be completely made up to 10 hours ahead and kept covered in the fridge. Not suitable for freezing.

Makes about 20–29, depending
on size of loaf

TO PREPARE AHEAD

**Prepare up to the end of step
2, cover the baking sheets
in clingfilm and keep in
the fridge for up to 3 days.
Freezes well assembled but
uncooked, for up to 1 month;
thaw before cooking.**

TO COOK IN THE AGA

**Bake on the floor of the
Roasting Oven for about 7–10
minutes, watching carefully,
until melted and golden
brown.**

Chèvre and Paprika Toasts

*Although these are good to serve with drinks, they can be offered
as a first course – simply use a larger French stick. If you cannot get
sun-dried tomato paste, use red pesto as an alternative.*

*1 thin French stick
butter, at room temperature, for
   spreading
about 4 tablespoons sun-dried
   tomato paste*

*about 225–300g (8–10 oz)
   chèvre (goat's cheese, the
   smaller the roll the better)
a little mild paprika
12–15 black olives, halved*

**Preheat the oven to 220°C/Fan 200°C/Gas 7. You will need
2 greased baking sheets.**

1 Slice the French stick into 5mm (¼ in) rounds and butter one side.
Arrange, buttered side down, on the baking sheets.
2 Spread a little of the sun-dried tomato paste on the plain side of the
bread. Slice the chèvre into slices about the thickness of a digestive
biscuit and arrange on top of the bread and tomato paste. Dust lightly
with a little paprika. Top each portion with half an olive, cut side down.
3 Bake in the preheated oven for about 8–10 minutes, or until the
cheese is melted and golden brown, and serve warm.

Tiny Quiche Lorraines

This is a quick, easy way to make a party quantity of bite-size quiches, and serve them hot. Making one large quiche in a Swiss roll tin, then cutting it out into miniature rounds is far quicker and less fiddly than making individual tiny quiches. For me, the cutting-out technique wins, hands down. Also, there is only pastry on the bottom of the little quiches with this method, so it's healthier and less fattening!

225g (8 oz) bought or home-made shortcrust pastry
a knob of butter
1 large onion, very finely chopped
2 tablespoons pesto, bought or home-made
300ml (10 fl oz) double cream

3 large eggs
2 tablespoons chopped fresh chives
75g (3 oz) Gruyère cheese, grated
salt and freshly ground black pepper

Preheat the oven to 200°C/Fan 180°C/Gas 6. Put a baking sheet in the oven to preheat to very hot. You will also need a shallow oblong Swiss roll tin about 28 x 18cm (11 x 7 in).

1 Roll out the pastry thinly and use to line the base and sides of the tin. Trim away and discard the excess pastry from the top rim of the tin. Prick the base of the pastry all over with a fork.

2 Heat the butter in a non-stick frying pan. Add the onion, and cook gently for about 10 minutes until the onion is softened but not coloured. Stir in the pesto. Remove from the heat and leave to cool.

3 In a bowl combine the cream, eggs, chives and half the cheese, and beat together with a wire whisk. Season well.

4 Spread the onion mixture over the base of the pastry. Carefully pour in the quiche filling, and sprinkle with the remaining cheese.

5 Slide on to the hot baking sheet in the preheated oven and bake for about 30 minutes, or until puffed and golden, turning halfway through.

6 Leave the tin on top of a wire rack to cool. When cool enough to handle, cut the quiche into rounds using a 3cm (1¼ in) plain cutter, or larger if you like.

7 When ready to serve, arrange the mini quiches on a baking sheet and return to the hot oven (at the same temperature as before) for about 10–15 minutes, or until tinged golden and piping hot.

Makes about 40

TO PREPARE AHEAD

Make the large quiche and cut into rounds (up to the end of step 6) about 48 hours before serving. Cover and refrigerate. Then continue from step 7. Freeze at the end of step 6 for up to 2 months.

TO COOK IN THE AGA

At step 2, fry the onion on the Boiling Plate. Cover and transfer to the Simmering Oven for 10 minutes for the onion to soften. At the end of step 5, slide on to the floor of the Roasting Oven and bake for about 25–30 minutes or until puffed and golden, turning halfway through. If necessary slide in the cold plain shelf on the second set of runners. At step 7, arrange the mini quiches on a baking sheet and bake on the floor of the Roasting Oven for 10–15 minutes, or until tinged golden and piping hot.

Makes about 30

TO PREPARE AHEAD

These can be assembled up to the end of step 3 about 8 hours ahead. Cook and serve immediately. Not suitable for freezing.

TO COOK IN THE AGA

Bake on the grid shelf on the floor of the Roasting Oven for about 10 minutes.

Smoked Mackerel and Spring Onion Bites

These lovely warm canapés are perfect to go with drinks before supper or for a drinks party. They take very little time and effort, and will be enjoyed by all!

1 x 375g packet ready-rolled
  shortcrust pastry
a knob of butter
2 bunches spring onions, finely
  sliced
100g (4 oz) smoked mackerel,
  skin removed, flesh flaked
2 heaped tablespoons full-fat
  crème fraîche

3 heaped tablespoons creamed
  horseradish
salt and freshly ground black
  pepper
75g (3 oz) mature Cheddar,
  grated
a little paprika

Preheat the oven to 200°C/Fan 180°C/Gas 6.

1 Roll out the pastry round to about the thickness of a £1 coin. Using a 5cm (2 in) cutter, cut out about 30 rounds. Arrange on a baking sheet greased or lined with non-stick paper.
2 Melt the butter in a small saucepan, add the spring onions, and cook over a medium heat for about 5 minutes, or until soft. Set aside to cool.
3 Put 1 teaspoon of spring onion on to each pastry base. In a bowl, mix together the smoked mackerel, crème fraîche and horseradish, and season with pepper and a little salt. Spoon on top of the spring onions and sprinkle with a little grated cheese. Dust with paprika.
4 Bake in the preheated oven for about 10–12 minutes, or until golden brown and the pastry is cooked. Serve warm.

Mary Berry's Stress-free Kitchen

Fresh Herb Dip

So easy and yet so delicious, this takes no time at all. It is a great bonus that, if you grow your own herbs, it is cheap too. Parsley, basil and chives are essential, but you can omit the others if preferred, or if they are unavailable. The dip is also good thinned down as a sauce (see page 201), or as a side dish with fish or a baked potato.

see page 201

Serves 10 as a dip

TO PREPARE AHEAD
Prepare up to the end of step 2, cover and keep in the fridge for 2–3 days. Not suitable for freezing

1 small bunch fresh parsley
3 sprigs fresh basil
2 sprigs fresh thyme
1 sprig fresh tarragon
1 small bunch fresh chives
1 x 125g carton full-fat cream cheese
1 x 200ml carton half-fat crème fraîche

1–2 small garlic cloves, crushed
6 tablespoons 'light', low-calorie mayonnaise
a pinch of caster sugar
2 tablespoons lemon juice
salt and freshly ground black pepper

1 Take the stalks off the herbs and discard. Chop the chives finely.
2 Put the parsley, basil, thyme and tarragon in the processor, and process until finely chopped. Add the cheese, crème fraîche, garlic, mayonnaise, sugar and lemon juice, and whizz again until smooth. If you do not have a processor, chop the herbs finely and mix in a bowl with the other ingredients until evenly combined. Season to taste.
3 Just before serving, stir in the chives. Serve with breadsticks, crudités or tortilla chips.

Little Smoked Haddock Fishcakes with Quail's Eggs

These stunning warm canapés are not difficult to make and most of the work can be done ahead of time.

12 quail's eggs, hard-boiled, shelled and quartered

FISHCAKES
350g (12 oz) undyed smoked haddock, skin on
350g (12 oz) King Edward potatoes, peeled
2 tablespoons 'light', low-calorie mayonnaise
1 tablespoon Dijon mustard
1 large egg yolk
½ bunch fresh dill, 6 sprigs reserved, the remainder chopped

1 teaspoon lemon juice
salt and freshly ground black pepper
75g (3 oz) fresh white breadcrumbs
a little sunflower oil, for frying

DILL SAUCE
4 tablespoons 'light', low-calorie mayonnaise
1 teaspoon lemon juice
½ bunch fresh dill, chopped
salt and freshly ground black pepper

Preheat the oven to 190°C/Fan 170°C/Gas 5.

1 First make the fishcakes. Put the haddock on to a piece of buttered foil, skin-side up. Cover the fish with foil and seal the edges. Slide on to a baking sheet and cook in the preheated oven for 12 minutes, or until just cooked. Leave to cool.
2 Cut the potatoes into 2cm (¾ in) cubes, put into a saucepan and cover with cold salted water. Bring up to the boil, then simmer for about 15 minutes, or until soft. Drain and mash the potatoes, and leave to cool for about 10 minutes.
3 Peel the skin from the cold haddock and discard. Break up the fish into large chunks with your hands, and add to the mashed potato with some of the fish juices from the foil. Add the mayonnaise, mustard, egg yolk, dill and lemon juice, and mix well. Season with pepper, and check for flavour: it is unlikely to need salt as the smoked haddock is usually on the salty side.

Mary Berry's Stress-free Kitchen

4 Shape the mixture into 24 mini cakes about the size of a £2 coin, 1.5cm (⅝ in) deep. Scatter the breadcrumbs on to a plate and coat each fishcake in breadcrumbs. Chill in the fridge while you make the sauce.

5 For the sauce, mix together the mayonnaise, lemon juice and dill, and season well.

6 Heat a little sunflower oil in a large frying pan. Add the fishcakes and brown for 1–2 minutes on each side, or until lightly golden.

Preheat the oven to 200C/Fan 180/Gas 6.

7 To serve, place the fishcakes on a baking sheet and reheat in the preheated oven for 5 minutes, or until heated through. Leave to cool for 2–3 minutes, then place on a serving platter.

8 Spoon a small amount of the sauce onto each cake, and top with a quarter of a quail's egg and a tiny piece of the reserved dill. Serve warm.

Pesto and Cheese Focaccia Eats

These are attractive served in a pile with a dip or a variety of dips (see Fresh Herb Dip, page 9). They are equally good with soup or salads. We are so lucky with the huge variety of different-flavoured breads we can buy. For a change try this recipe with olive bread or sun-dried tomato bread.

1 ready-to-bake focaccia bread
50g (2 oz) soft butter
1 fat garlic clove, crushed
50g (2 oz) Parmesan, grated

2 tablespoons green pesto, bought or home-made
2 tablespoons chopped fresh parsley

Preheat the oven to 200°C/Fan 180°C/Gas 6.

1 Put the focaccia on a baking sheet.
2 Mix together all the remaining ingredients and spread over the focaccia base.
3 Bake in the preheated oven for about 10–12 minutes, or until golden brown.
4 Slice the focaccia into 20 small squares and serve warm.

TO PREPARE AHEAD
This can be made the day before up to the end of step 2 and cooked to serve or reheated after step 4 in a moderate oven till warm. At the end of step 4, freeze for up to 2 months.

TO COOK IN THE AGA
Slide the baking sheet on to the second set of runners in the Roasting Oven and bake for about 10 minutes.

Miniature Bangers and Mash

Prepare to the end of step 4 up to 1 day before. Cover and keep in the fridge. Bring back to room temperature, then continue from step 5. To freeze at the end of step 4, pack the sausages in a single layer in a freezer-proof container. Freeze for up to 1 month.

Cook the sausages (if raw) on non-stick baking paper in a roasting dish on the floor of the Roasting Oven until cooked and brown. At step 5, reheat in the Roasting Oven on the top set of runners for about 5 minutes.

Rather than boiling only 2 small potatoes to fill the sausages, why not boil extra and use the leftovers for supper? Don't forget to warn the guests if the sausages are very hot. When making food for a drinks party, don't forget old favourites like devils-on-horseback (prunes wrapped in bacon).

20 cocktail sausages
  (Marks and Spencer and
  some supermarkets sell
  them ready cooked)
2 small potatoes, cooked and
  mashed

salt and freshly ground black
  pepper
a little grated Parmesan
a little paprika

1 Grill the sausages (if raw), turning once or twice until cooked and evenly brown. Allow the sausages to become completely cold. Make a slit down the length of each one to form an opening (this is easier if they are cold).

Preheat the oven to 200°C/Fan 180°C/Gas 6.

2 Ensure that the potatoes are very well seasoned. Turn into a piping bag fitted with a plain narrow nozzle. (If you prefer, use a teaspoon.)
3 Hold a sausage, squeezing the ends gently together, and pipe or spoon the potato into the gap.
4 Sprinkle the sausages with Parmesan and dust with paprika. Arrange on a baking sheet.
5 Reheat in the preheated oven for about 10 minutes, or until piping hot.

Starters

Most of this selection of stress-free starters or first-course recipes are capable of being made ahead and reheated (if appropriate), as I recognise that most people want to get things ready beforehand to avoid last-minute panics! Soups are always very handy as they can be prepared well in advance and frozen, as can the stocks for soups (wonderful made in the Simmering Oven of the Aga), but as this is a book of stress-free recipes, don't feel in the least guilty about choosing stock cubes or powder instead, or, indeed, stock sold in cartons. (Soups are also good for lunch, which is why I always have some available, and why I'm actually pleased if I have some left over.)

Cold dishes, of course, can also be prepared in advance. Some of the recipes here use good bought-in ingredients, like the antipasto platter, and many don't even need any cooking. I'm quite keen on cold first courses, as I can lay them out on each plate setting, where they will look pretty and welcoming for when my guests come into sit down. (Another bonus is that these cold starters can come up to room temperature after being in the fridge.) Leave the plates covered with clingfilm until the last moment, and if there are eager pets in the house keep the door firmly closed! In winter, though, warm or hot starters would be appreciated, so a few have been included.

For more starter ideas, see:

Roasted Pepper and Squash Soup

Serves 6

A perfect soup to keep in the fridge for 2–3 days, or to freeze. It has a lovely bright colour too. Serve with crusty bread rolls.

1 medium butternut squash, peeled, seeded and chopped into 4cm (1½ in) pieces
3 tablespoons olive oil
2 red peppers, halved and seeded
1 red chilli, seeded and finely chopped

2 garlic cloves, crushed
1 x 400g can chopped tomatoes
1.5 litres (2¾ pints) chicken or vegetable stock
juice of 2 large oranges
salt and freshly ground black pepper

Preheat the oven to 200°C/Fan 180°C/Gas 6.

1 Put the squash pieces into a small roasting tin with 2 tablespoons of the oil and mix until the squash is coated. Arrange the halved peppers on top of the squash and roast in the preheated oven for about 30 minutes, or until the squash is just soft and the pepper skins are brown.

2 Carefully remove the hot peppers, place in a bowl, cover with clingfilm and leave to cool. When cool enough to handle, remove the clingfilm and peel the skins away from the flesh.

3 Heat a deep saucepan, add the cooked squash, skinned peppers, chilli and garlic, and fry for 2–3 minutes in the remaining oil. Add the tomatoes, stock and orange juice, bring up to the boil, season, cover with a lid and simmer for about 15 minutes.

4 Carefully ladle the soup into a processor and whizz until smooth (you will have to do this in batches), or use a hand blender.

5 Pour into a clean saucepan and reheat to serve. Check the seasoning.

TO PREPARE AHEAD

The completed soup can be made up to 2 days ahead and kept in the fridge. Freezes for up to 2 months.

TO COOK IN THE AGA

At step 1, roast the squash and peppers on the floor of the Roasting Oven for about 15 minutes, or until tender. At step 3, bring to the boil on the Boiling Plate, cover and transfer to the Simmering Oven, and cook for about 15 minutes, or until tender.

Watercress and Celeriac Soup

Serves 6

Celeriac is a late summer and winter vegetable with a wonderful flavour. It must be peeled fairly thickly as it is such a knobbly shape. As you peel it, pop the pieces in a little acidulated water (water with lemon juice added) to prevent it discolouring after peeling.

2 bunches watercress
65g (2¼ oz) butter
1 large onion, sliced
350g (12 oz) celeriac, peeled
  weight, cut into small cubes
40g (1½ oz) plain flour

1.2 litres (2 pints) chicken stock
salt and freshly ground black
  pepper
about 300ml (10 fl oz) milk,
  boiling
a little single cream

1 Wash the watercress but do not remove the stalks. Set aside. Trim off a small bunch of leaves to use for a garnish if not freezing.

2 Melt the butter in a saucepan and gently toss the onion and celeriac for about 3–4 minutes, not letting them brown. Add the flour, mix well, then add the stock and seasoning. Bring to the boil, then simmer, covered, for about 30 minutes until tender.

3 Add the watercress, with stalks, and simmer for a further 5 minutes. Purée the soup in a processor. Return the soup to the pan and add enough boiling milk to give it the required consistency to your liking; we like it about the thickness of double cream. Check the seasoning.

4 To serve, stir in a little cream and sprinkle each serving with the reserved, finely chopped watercress leaves. Do not keep the soup hot for any length of time, as it will go grey in colour.

TO PREPARE AHEAD

Complete to the end of step 3, cool quickly, then store in a sealed container in the fridge for up to 2 days. Reheat thoroughly to serve, but do not allow to boil. Freeze at the end of step 3 for up to 1 month.

TO COOK IN THE AGA

At step 2, cook the onion and celeriac on the Boiling Plate. Simmer on the Simmering Plate for 5 minutes, then transfer to the floor of the Simmering Oven, covered, for about 30 minutes, or until tender. At step 3, simmer on the Simmering Plate.

TO PREPARE AHEAD

This soup can be made (without the garnish) up to 2 days ahead and kept in the fridge. Freezes well without the garnish for up to 2 months.

TO COOK IN THE AGA

At step 2, bring to the boil on the Boiling Plate, then cover and transfer to the Simmering Oven for about 10–15 minutes, or until the vegetables are tender.

Kidney Bean Soup with Crispy Bacon Topping

A hearty soup made with store-cupboard ingredients, which immediately cuts out a lot of stress. Use beef, chicken or vegetable stock cubes for this quick recipe.

1–2 tablespoons olive oil
1 large onion, finely chopped
2 celery sticks, string removed, cut into small cubes
1 medium potato, cut into small cubes
1 x 400g can kidney beans, drained, washed and drained again

900ml (1½ pints) chicken or vegetable stock

GARNISH
6 rashers smoked streaky bacon
2 tablespoons single cream
2 tablespoons chopped fresh parsley

1 Heat the oil in a saucepan, add the onion and celery, and fry gently for about 5 minutes until they begin to soften.

2 Add the potato and beans to the pan and pour over the stock. Bring to the boil and simmer, covered, over a low heat for about 10 minutes, depending on size, or until the vegetables are just tender.

3 Purée the soup in a processor or blender until smooth. If too thick, thin down with a little more stock.

4 For the garnish, snip the bacon into small pieces and fry over a high heat until crisp. Swirl a little cream into the soup, then sprinkle over the parsley and crispy bacon bits.

Crab Cakes with Mild Chilli Sauce

Fresh and frozen crabmeat can be difficult to come by, so I use tinned. I found John West to be the best. The dipping sauce I use is Blue Dragon sweet chilli dipping sauce. I always make these cakes ahead, and reheat them so that there is no last-minute frying. Serve 1 crab cake per person as a starter or 2 per person as a main course.

450g (1 lb) fresh white crabmeat, or 3 x 170g cans John West white crabmeat, drained

2 tablespoons chopped fresh parsley

40g (1½ oz) cream crackers, finely crushed in a polythene bag with a rolling pin

1 large egg

2 tablespoons 'light', low-calorie mayonnaise

1–2 teaspoons Dijon mustard

2 tablespoons lemon juice

1 tablespoon sweet chilli dipping sauce

salt and freshly ground black pepper

a little sunflower oil for frying

CHILLI SAUCE

8 tablespoons sweet chilli dipping sauce

4 tablespoons full-fat crème fraîche

1 Measure the crabmeat into a bowl and mix with the parsley and cream crackers.

2 Break the egg into a small bowl and whisk in the mayonnaise, mustard, lemon juice and chilli sauce, and seasoning. Fold most of this mixture into the crabmeat but try not to break up the lumps of meat too much. (You may not need all the egg mixture, just enough to bind it all together.) Taste and add more seasoning if necessary.

3 Shape the mixture into 12 patties, lay them on a plate, cover with clingfilm and chill for at least 1 hour.

4 Mix together the sweet chilli sauce and crème fraîche, and keep in the fridge until needed.

5 Heat the sunflower oil in a large frying pan and cook the crab cakes for 2–3 minutes, or until hot all the way through, crisp and richly golden, turning once. Serve straight away with a spoonful of the cold sauce on the side of the plate.

TO PREPARE AHEAD

Fry the crab cakes the day before, then reheat them, uncovered, on a baking sheet in the oven preheated to 200°C/Fan 180°C/Gas 6 for about 10 minutes, or until hot through. Not suitable for freezing.

TO COOK IN THE AGA

Fry the crab cakes ahead on the Boiling Plate, then reheat them, uncovered, on non-stick baking paper on the second set of runners in the Roasting Oven for about 7–10 minutes, or until hot right through.

TO PREPARE AHEAD

Prepare the plates up to the end of step 3 a few hours ahead , and keep them covered with clingfilm. If you want to prepare the dish well ahead, prepare the melon and figs separately, and add the ham when finally assembling just before serving. Not suitable for freezing.

Fresh Figs with Parma Ham and Melon

Choose ripe figs for this recipe but avoid handling them too much, otherwise they will lose their cloudy bloom, like black grapes when touched. Home-grown figs in the summer are shiny, so there is no problem. To tell when a melon is ripe, gently press the top at the opposite end to the stalk: if it is softish, and smells ripe and sweet, it will be ripe. If buying a few days ahead, allow to ripen out of the fridge in a warm kitchen. Avoid blemished melons unless you are making a fruit salad and they are a bargain!

1 ripe Cantaloupe melon
8 slices Parma ham

4 figs, halved lengthways
through the stem

1 Slice the melon in quarters lengthways. Remove the flesh from the skin by running your knife between them. Chop the flesh into pieces and divide between 4 plates, making a pile in the centre of each.

2 Place 2 pieces of ham on top of each pile of melon, curling the ham with your fingers to give a large spiral shape so it is piled high and not flat.

3 Put 1 fig half next to each pile of melon. Cut the remaining halves halfway through the stem so that they are still joined at the base, and open them out slightly to form a 'V'. Arrange these opposite the fig halves on the other side of the melon pile on each plate so that the melon is in the middle with the ham on top, the fig half on the left and the 'V' fig on the right.

4 Serve chilled.

Prepare up to the end of step 6, cover in clingfilm and keep in the fridge for up to 48 hours. Freeze at the end of step 6, wrapped in clingfilm, for up to 1 month.

TO COOK IN THE AGA
Cook the soufflés on the roasting sheet on the grid shelf on the floor of the Roasting Oven for about 15–20 minutes, or until golden and well risen. After 10 minutes turn round and slide the cold sheet on the second set of runners.

Reheat in the gratin dish with the sauce in same position with the cold sheet for about 15 minutes.

Swiss Double Soufflés

This makes a delicious lunch or supper dish, served with crusty bread and a mixed leaf salad.

SOUFFLÉ
100g (4 oz) leaf spinach
300ml (10 fl oz) milk
40g (1½ oz) butter
40g (1½ oz) plain flour
salt and freshly ground black
  pepper
a pinch of nutmeg
50g (2 oz) Gruyère cheese,
  grated

3 large eggs, separated
50g (2 oz) Parmesan, grated

PESTO SAUCE
300ml (10 fl oz) pouring double
  cream
2 tablespoons green pesto,
  bought or home-made

Preheat the oven to 200°C/Fan 180°C/Gas 6. You will need 6 small ramekins (9 x 4cm/3½ x 1½ in), well buttered, and a shallow gratin dish, large enough to hold all 6 soufflés without touching each other, also well buttered. Have ready a kettle of boiling water.

1 Wash the spinach thoroughly and shred finely. Tip into a pan, pour over the milk and bring to the boil. Stir well and set aside.
2 Melt the butter in a generous-sized saucepan over the heat. Remove the pan and blend in the flour. Return to the heat and cook the roux for 1 minute. Gradually blend in the spinach and milk, stirring all the time. Continue to stir until the sauce is thick and smooth and has just come to the boil. Remove the pan from the heat, season, and add the nutmeg and Gruyère cheese. Stir well to combine, then, still off the heat, fold in the egg yolks.
3 In a clean bowl, whisk the egg whites until they are stiff. Fold carefully into the sauce mixture.
4 Spoon the mixture into the buttered ramekins. Place them in a small roasting tin and pour boiling water into the tin to come halfway up the dishes.
5 Cook in the preheated oven for about 15–20 minutes, or until golden brown and springy to the touch. You may need to turn them round after about 10 minutes. Remove from the oven and leave the soufflés to cool in the ramekins for 5–10 minutes to shrink back a little.

6 Sprinkle half the Parmesan in the bottom of the buttered gratin dish. Run the blade of a small palette knife round the edge of the little soufflés, then unmould them carefully and lay them in the gratin dish so that they do not touch.

7 Season the pouring cream and stir in the pesto. Pour around the soufflés in the dish. Sprinkle the remaining Parmesan over the top.

8 Return to the hot oven for about 15–20 minutes, or until the soufflés have puffed up and are golden. Don't overcook, otherwise the sauce may separate. Serve immediately.

Serves 4

Prepare ahead to the end of step 5 up to 12 hours in advance, keeping separate the griddled toast, cooked mushrooms and sliced cheese. Not suitable for freezing.

TO COOK IN THE AGA

Slide the baking sheet on to the top set of runners in the Roasting Oven and cook for about 8 minutes.

Mushroom Bruschettas with Taleggio and Fresh Pesto Dressing

This is delicious as a starter or light lunch dish. If you can't get hold of the Italian Taleggio cheese, use Swiss Reblochon or any semi-soft or blue cheese that you might have left.

100g (4 oz) Taleggio cheese
4 thickish slices good brown
  bread
about 8 tablespoons olive oil
a knob of butter
4 large flat Portobello
  mushrooms, stalks removed

salt and freshly ground black
  pepper
a little paprika
6 tablespoons fresh basil pesto,
  bought or home-made

Preheat the oven to 220°C/Fan 200°C/Gas 7.

1 First, put the cheese in the freezer for 2–3 hours. (This makes it easier to slice thinly later.)

2 Use a round 9cm (3½ in) cutter to cut out 4 rounds from the bread (they should be slightly smaller than the diameter of the mushrooms), and brush each side lightly with a little oil. Toast in a griddle pan until golden brown. Set aside.

3 Heat a large frying pan over a high heat, then add 3 tablespoons oil and the butter. Season the mushrooms generously and add to the pan. Flatten slightly, and cover with a lid for 2–3 minutes, or until cooked on one side. Turn over, cover with the lid and cook in the steam for a further 2–3 minutes, or until cooked. Remove the lid and cook to drive off any liquid in the pan. Remove the mushrooms and set aside.

4 Take the cheese out of the freezer and cut into thin slices, enough to cover the mushrooms.

5 To cook, arrange the griddled bread on a baking sheet, top each with 1 mushroom and 1 slice of cheese, and sprinkle with paprika.

6 Cook in the preheated oven for about 8–10 minutes. Keep an eye on the bruschettas, and remove when the cheese is beginning to melt.

7 While the bruschettas are cooking, mix the pesto with the remaining olive oil, about 4 tablespoons, to give a pouring consistency.

8 Arrange the bruschettas on a hot serving plate and drizzle the pesto over the mushrooms and the plate in a zigzag pattern. Serve hot.

Antipasto of Continental Meats

Choose meats that you enjoy most. If serving as a main course, add some cheeses too, and perhaps complement the Parma ham with some fresh figs. Look out for vacuum packs of mixed sliced continental meats, which are useful if you are making smaller platters because you won't have to have each individual meat sliced and weighed out separately at the deli counter.

175g (6 oz) mixed olives
1 x 175g jar artichokes in oil
4 tablespoons balsamic vinegar
4 tablespoons olive oil
6 slices pastrami

12 slices salami
6 slices Parma ham
12 thin slices chorizo
1 x 50g bag rocket

1 Decant the drained olives and artichokes into 2 small oval ramekins.
2 Measure the vinegar and oil into a third oval ramekin, then set all the ramekins near the centre of a large round platter, in a triangle shape.
3 Arrange the meats separately between the gaps, curling the Parma ham and pastrami so they are loosely draped on the platter.
4 Place the rocket in the middle of the platter, and serve with warm Italian bread.

TO PREPARE AHEAD
The meats can be arranged up to 12 hours ahead on a large platter that will fit into the fridge. Cover with clingfilm. Not suitable for freezing.

Serves 6

Trio of Prawns

This starter, a plate of three different prawn recipes, looks very impressive, but is remarkably easy to make, with no cooking at all. If you prefer not to have the prawn cocktail on a circle of brown bread, serve slices of buttered bread separately.

PRAWN COCKTAIL
75g (3 oz) North Atlantic shelled
   cooked prawns
6 tablespoons full-fat
   mayonnaise
1 tablespoon tomato ketchup
1 generous teaspoon creamed
   horseradish
salt and freshly ground black
   pepper
6 slices seeded brown bread, cut
   into 7cm (2¾ in) rounds and
   spread thinly with butter
1 Little Gem lettuce, finely
   shredded
1 tablespoon chopped fresh
   parsley

6 small lemon wedges

PRAWNS WITH CHILLI SAUCE
75g (3 oz) North Atlantic shelled
   cooked prawns
6 dessertspoons sweet chilli
   dipping sauce
1 tablespoon chopped fresh
   coriander
1 Little Gem lettuce

PRAWNS WITH AÏOLI
1 small garlic clove, crushed
6 dessertspoons mayonnaise
6 large king prawns, head and
   shell left on

1 First of all, pat dry all the prawns with kitchen paper so they are not wet. Keep each group separate.
2 To make the prawn cocktail, mix together the mayonnaise, ketchup and horseradish in a bowl, and season. Stir in the prawns. Arrange the brown bread on individual plates and top each round of bread with a little shredded lettuce. Top with the prawns and sprinkle with a little parsley. Put 1 lemon wedge beside the bread.
3 To make the chilli prawns, put the prawns in a bowl and stir in the chilli dipping sauce and most of the coriander. Arrange 2 Little Gem leaves per plate next to the prawn cocktail. Divide the chilli prawns into 6 portions and spoon into the leaves. Sprinkle with the remaining coriander.
4 To make the prawns with aïoli, mix the crushed garlic with the mayonnaise, and season well. Peel the shells from the prawns, leaving the head and peeled body attached. Arrange 1 prawn per plate with 1 teaspoon of aïoli beside it. Serve at room temperature.

Mary Berry's Stress-free Kitchen

Double Smoked Trout Brandade with Horseradish

Serves 8 (cuts into 16 wedges)

TO PREPARE AHEAD
Make to the end of step 4 up to 24 hours ahead and keep in the fridge. Not suitable for freezing.

This is a cross between a pâté and a terrine, with plenty of texture. Sliced cold-smoked trout is sold in vacuum packs, without skin, and is similar to smoked salmon. Hot-smoked whole trout fillets are lightly cooked and taste like lightly smoked fish. They are also without skin. You can buy whole smoked small trout, and skin and bone them yourself.

about 150g (5 oz) sliced
  cold-smoked trout
½ cucumber
200g (7 oz) full-fat cream cheese
250g (9 oz) hot-smoked trout
  fillets (4 fillets)
up to 1 tablespoon creamed
  horseradish (depending on the
  strength of sauce)
4 drops of Tabasco sauce
1 small bunch fresh chives,
  snipped

salt and freshly ground black
  pepper

TO SERVE
1 x 170g bag lamb's lettuce
a little salad dressing (see the
  vinaigrette recipe in Grainy
  Mustard and Herb Potato
  Salad, p.181)
8 lemon wedges

You will need a 20cm (8 in) round sandwich tin, lined with clingfilm.

1 Cover the base of the tin with a single layer of the cold-smoked trout slices.

2 Peel the cucumber with a potato peeler and cut in half lengthways. Remove the seeds with a teaspoon and discard. Chop the flesh into very small dice.

3 Measure the cream cheese and half the hot-smoked trout fillets into a processor and whizz until smooth. If you do not have a processor, chop half the trout fillets finely with a knife and mix with the cream cheese in a bowl to give a smooth paste. Scrape into a clean bowl. Roughly flake the remaining trout and fold in, together with the cucumber dice, the horseradish, Tabasco, chives and some black pepper. Check the seasoning.

4 Spoon the pâté mixture into the prepared tin and level the top. Cover with clingfilm and leave overnight in the fridge to firm up.

5 Turn out the brandade on to a round platter. Put in the freezer for 1 hour before serving, which makes it easier to slice.

6 To serve, cut carefully into 16 wedges. Arrange the lamb's lettuce on individual plates and dress it. Place 1 wedge of pâté alongside the lettuce and a second wedge diagonally across the first. Serve with the lemon wedges.

Mary Berry's Stress-free Kitchen

Fish

Fish is rich in protein, low in fat and carbohydrate, and we should all be eating more of it. However, we must always be aware that some species are severely under threat because of over-fishing. In the recipes here, I have only used commonly available fish, and fish that are sustainable. I tend not to buy fish from warmer seas on the other side of the world as I think they lack flavour (and certainly freshness) by the time they reach us. They usually only require grilling whole, too, which hardly merits a recipe.

Fish takes very little cooking, which cuts down on time, energy and stress. For the most stress-free fish preparation, cultivate your local fishmonger, and he will be able to do all your scaling, skinning, boning and filleting for you. Fishmongers may be in decline, sadly, but I'm very pleased to see that our supermarkets are now offering excellent fish, and many fish counters boast interested and knowledgeable staff.

The recipes here range from grilled and roasted fillets, to fishcakes and a homely supper-type fish pie. Buy fish only when very fresh, and cook it that day or the next. Some fish can even be cooked partly the night before, such as the sea bass, which is a huge bonus in terms of time, stress levels and fishy smells in the kitchen when your guests arrive ...

For more fish ideas, see:

Roasted Crusted Salmon Fillet

A great hot party dish. The salmon is pre-cut into portions before cooking, making it so easy to serve. If time is short, you can always buy a jar of onion marmalade instead of making it yourself. Onions go really well with the salmon and make it very moist. The hint of sweet red peppers adds a dash of colour.

Peppadew peppers are small bell peppers from South Africa, found in jars in good delis and supermarkets. They are available hot or mild, and we like the mild ones best. Once opened, keep in the fridge, and use them in Five-Spice Mango Chicken (page 191), Chilled Gazpacho Chicken (page 192), salads or pasta, or stuffed with cream cheese.

TO PREPARE AHEAD
Prepare up to the end of step 4 up to 24 hours ahead, cover with clingfilm and put in the fridge. Freeze at the end of step 4 for up to a month wrapped in foil.

TO COOK IN THE AGA
Fry the onion marmalade on the Boiling Plate for 2–3 minutes, cover and transfer to the Simmering Oven for about 1 hour. Drive off the wetness from the onion on the Boiling Plate before adding the vinegar. Cook the salmon in the centre of the Roasting Oven for about 20–25 minutes.

1 x 1kg (2½ lb) side of salmon, with skin on
salt and freshly ground black pepper

ONION MARMALADE
1 tablespoon olive oil
700g (1½ lb) onions, thinly sliced
1 tablespoon balsamic vinegar

CRUMB TOPPING
1 small bunch fresh basil, chopped
20 mild peppadew peppers, from a jar, drained and thinly sliced
50g (2 oz) Parmesan, coarsely grated
50g (2 oz) fresh white breadcrumbs
finely grated zest of 1 lemon

Preheat the oven to 220°C/Fan 200°C/Gas 7. Grease or line a baking sheet.

1 First make the onion marmalade. Heat the oil in a large frying pan or saucepan over a medium heat. Add the onions, stir well and season. Cook slowly, covered, until the onions are very soft, stirring from time to time. This will take about 1 hour, during which time the onions will become darker, and sticky and soft.

2 Add the vinegar, and bring to the boil to reduce any liquid. Set aside to become cold.

3 Sit the salmon fillet on the prepared baking sheet. With a sharp knife, cut through the flesh of the fish until the knife touches the skin (but do not cut through the skin). Cut into 8 even-sized pieces. Season.

4 Spread the cold onion marmalade over the salmon fillet and sprinkle with the basil. In a bowl mix together the peppers, Parmesan, breadcrumbs and lemon zest, and press on top of the salmon.

5 Bake in the preheated oven for about 20–25 minutes (depending on the thickness of the salmon), or until the flesh is cooked and has turned opaque pink. Check by poking the centre of the fish with a knife. Allow to rest for about 10 minutes, covered with foil.

6 To serve, cut between the slices as far as the skin and lift off with a fish slice. Serve hot.

Thai Salmon

This truly simple recipe evolved from an idea passed on to me in the time-honoured fashion of a few scribbles on the back of an old envelope.

Timing is all-important here. As Marco Pierre White said in his interview with Sue Lawley on Desert Island Discs, one of the reasons he did not allow any conversation between staff in his kitchen was that 5 seconds too long could ruin the cooking of a piece of fish.

Red Thai curry paste is available from good delicatessens and supermarkets, where it is usually to be found with the herbs and spices. I have suggested a scant teaspoon of the Thai paste, but add more if you like.

2 x 300g (10 oz) fresh salmon
  fillets, skin left on
olive oil
salt and freshly ground black
  pepper

SAUCE
1 x 2.5cm (1 in) piece fresh
  ginger root

1 tablespoon olive oil
1 small garlic clove, crushed
1 small orange
1 scant teaspoon red Thai curry
  paste
1 x 300ml carton full-fat crème
  fraîche

TO PREPARE AHEAD

Thai salmon is best grilled to order, although you can make the sauce ahead. Not suitable for freezing.

TO COOK IN THE AGA

For step 2, use the Simmering Plate to soften the onion. After adding the garlic, cover and transfer to the floor of the Simmering Oven for 10 minutes. At step 3, bring to the boil on the Boiling Plate. At step 4, put a ridged grill pan to heat up on the Simmering Plate. Transfer to the Boiling Plate and cook the salmon as above. Reheat the sauce gently on the Simmering Plate.

1 Cut each salmon fillet in half lengthways, brush both sides with oil, and season.

2 Using a potato peeler, peel the ginger and cut into needle-thin strips lengthways. Soften in the oil in a large-based saucepan for 5 minutes, then add the garlic. Stir well and cover and cook over medium heat for about 10 minutes until soft. (The reason for using a large pan is that it is quicker to reduce the sauce later.)

3 Remove the zest from the orange using a zester, then squeeze the juice. Add the Thai paste to the ginger and garlic mixture, and stir well. Next add the orange juice and zest, and lastly the crème fraîche. Bring to the boil, simmer for 2–3 minutes, and add salt to taste. If necessary, boil further to reduce to a creamy consistency. Keep warm.

4 Heat a non-stick ridged grill pan or frying pan on the hob. Put the salmon, flesh side down, on to the hot grill pan and cook for 30–45 seconds, then turn on to the skin side and continue cooking for about 3½ minutes (about 3½–5 minutes total), according to the thickness of the salmon. Watch it like a hawk. (If you like your fish barely cooked, do not be tempted to leave it longer, as you can always return it to the pan, but there is nothing you can do if it is overcooked.)

5 To serve, pour a little warm sauce on to each plate, place a fillet of salmon to one side of it, and then serve the rest of the sauce separately.

Trompretti Pasta with Crab and Potted Shrimps

Trompretti is usually a fresh funnel-shaped pasta with crinkly edges. It is very pretty, but the dish works just as well with any other fresh pasta. If you can get fresh pasta, this becomes the quickest pasta dish you will ever make. If you are lucky enough to have a good source of fresh crabmeat, use this instead of canned. You may like to increase the chilli to make it hotter.

300g (10 oz) fresh trompretti
  pasta
150g (5 oz) frozen peas
salt and freshly ground black
  pepper
2 x 57g cartons potted shrimps
½ red chilli, finely chopped

1 x 170g can white crabmeat,
  well drained
1 x 200ml carton pouring double
  cream
juice of ½ lemon
2 tablespoons chopped fresh
  parsley

1 Cook the pasta and peas together in a large saucepan of boiling salted water for 3 minutes or according to the packet instructions. Drain well.

2 Open the cartons of shrimps and lift as much butter as you can from them, reserving the shrimps for later. Melt this butter in a non-stick frying pan. Add the chilli, crabmeat and cream and bring to the boil. Season with black pepper.

3 Add the cooked pasta and peas to the boiling cream, along with the lemon juice. Toss together and tip into a warm serving bowl.

4 Quickly toss the shrimps in the empty (and unwashed) hot frying pan for about a minute just to heat through and sprinkle them and the parsley over the pasta. Serve at once.

Serves 4

TO PREPARE AHEAD
So easy, just gather up the ingredients and make in 5 minutes. Not suitable for freezing.

TO COOK IN THE AGA
Cook on the Boiling Plate.

Smoked Haddock Coulibiac

A good family supper or dinner party dish, this is easy to serve with a green leaf salad. You can now buy puff pastry made with real butter, which is delicious but a little softer to handle.

TO PREPARE AHEAD

Make 24 hours ahead up to the end of step 7 but do not brush the outside with the egg. Cover with clingfilm and keep in the fridge. Brush with beaten egg before cooking. Freeze at the end of step 7 for up to 2 months, but before brushing with the beaten egg.

TO COOK IN THE AGA

Bake on the floor of the Roasting Oven for about 25–30 minutes.

1 x 500g packet puff pastry
1 large egg, beaten

SMOKED HADDOCK FILLING
450g (1 lb) undyed smoked
 haddock fillet, skin on
50g (2 oz) butter
1 large onion, chopped
225g (8 oz) chestnut mushrooms,
 quartered
2 teaspoons curry powder
75g (3 oz) long-grain rice
2 good tablespoons chopped
 fresh parsley

salt and freshly ground black
 pepper
2 large eggs, hard-boiled, shelled
 and quartered

EASY MANGO SAUCE
1 x 200ml carton crème fraîche
4 generous tablespoons mango
 chutney
2 tablespoons chopped fresh
 parsley

1 First, put the haddock in a pan and cover with cold water. Bring to the boil, covered, and remove from the heat. Leave undisturbed for about 15 minutes to allow to cool (do not remove the lid). The haddock will finish cooking in the residual heat.

2 Melt the butter in a pan, add the onion and cook over a medium heat for about 10 minutes, or until soft. Add the mushrooms and toss over a high heat for a few moments. Sprinkle in the curry powder and cook for 1 minute more, stirring.

3 Once the haddock is cooked, lift from the pan, using a slotted spoon, and set aside. Add the rice to the fish liquid. If not quite covered, add a little more water. Boil according to the packet instructions, usually about 12 minutes, or until cooked. Drain well.

4 Flake the fish into fairly large pieces, removing any bones. Discard the skin.

5 In a bowl mix together the drained rice, fish, curried vegetables and parsley, and season to taste. Set aside until cold.

Preheat the oven to 200°C/Fan 180°C/Gas 6. Line a baking sheet with non-stick baking paper.

6 Roll out the pastry into a 35cm (14 in) square, and lift on to the prepared baking sheet. Spoon half the rice mixture down one long side of the pastry, leaving a 5cm (2 in) border at the near edges. Arrange the hard-boiled egg quarters on top of the rice and top with the remaining rice mixture.

7 Brush the outer edges of the pastry square with the beaten egg Lift the loose half of the pastry over the rice, bringing the long edges together, and press down on the 5cm (2 in) border to seal the edges. Decorate the coulibiac with pastry leaves and brush with the beaten egg.

8 Bake in the preheated oven for about 30 minutes, or until the pastry is golden brown.

9 Mix together the sauce ingredients. Serve the hot coulibiac in slices with the sauce.

Salmon and Fennel Fish Pie

This is a fish pie for a very special occasion. Adding ricotta cheese to the mashed potato lightens the texture and gives an interesting flavour. The recipe provided here makes enough for 12 people, but it can easily be altered to serve 6: simply halve all the quantities.

700g (1½lb) fresh fennel bulbs
300ml (10 fl oz) dry white wine
about 900ml (1½ pints) hot milk
100g (4 oz) butter
100g (4 oz) plain flour
salt and freshly ground black pepper
1.4kg (3 lb) salmon fillets, skinned and cut into 1cm (½ in) pieces
2 tablespoons chopped fresh dill

8 eggs, hard-boiled and cut into eighths

TOPPING
1.6kg (3½ lb) King Edward potatoes (weight before peeling), peeled and cut into large chunks
500g (1 lb 2 oz) ricotta cheese
100g (4 oz) Parmesan, grated
about 8 tablespoons milk

Preheat the oven to 200°C/Fan 180°C/Gas 6. You will need 1 shallow ovenproof dish, capacity 1.4 litres (2½ pints), about 28 x 23 x 5cm (11 x 9 x 2 in).

1 For the topping, cook the potatoes in boiling salted water until tender. Drain well.

2 While the potatoes are cooking, cut the fennel bulbs in half from top to bottom, and remove and discard the core. Cut into quarters and then slice in horseshoe shapes. Put into a small pan with the wine, and simmer until the fennel is soft, about 10 minutes. Drain the fennel, reserving the liquid, and make up to 1.1 litres (2 pints) with the milk.

3 Next make the sauce. Melt the butter in a medium pan, add the flour and stir to mix. Gradually add the milk and fennel liquid, stirring continuously and allowing to thicken. Season well, bring to the boil, and simmer for 2–3 minutes. Then add the salmon pieces and cook for a further 2–3 minutes. Stir in the fennel and dill, check the seasoning, and

TO PREPARE AHEAD
Prepare the pie(s) to the end of step 4. Cover with clingfilm and keep in the fridge for up to 1 day. Not suitable for freezing.

TO COOK IN THE AGA
At step 5, bake on the grid shelf on the floor of the Roasting Oven for about 30 minutes until the potato is crisp and golden, and the pie is piping hot.

remove from the heat. Spread the sauce into the dish or dishes. Scatter the eggs over the top, pressing down gently.

4 Mash the potatoes until smooth. Stir in the ricotta cheese and half the Parmesan, adding enough milk to create a creamy texture. Season well. Spoon over the sauce, spreading the potatoes right to the edge of the dish. Sprinkle with the remaining Parmesan.

5 Bake in the preheated oven for about 30–35 minutes, or until cooked through, brown, crisp and piping hot. If using 2 dishes, change round the position of the dishes halfway through the cooking time if necessary.

Char-Grilled Sea Bass on a Bed of Vegetables

Supper in one dish. Prepare the vegetables and fish ahead, leaving only a salad to make on the day.

700g (1½ lb) new potatoes,
  scrubbed
1 large onion, cut into wedges
olive oil
1 garlic clove, crushed
salt and freshly ground black
  pepper
4 large tomatoes, skinned,
  quartered and seeded

4 red peppers, cut in half and
  seeded
50g (2 oz) black olives in oil,
  drained
6 sea bass fillets, with the skin
  left on
chopped fresh parsley and basil

Preheat the oven to 200°C/Fan 180°C/Gas 6, and preheat the grill. You will need a 38 x 25cm (15 x 10 in) ovenproof dish, lightly buttered.

1 Boil the potatoes and onion in salted water until the potatoes are only just done. Drain and cut the potatoes into even pieces about 2.5cm (1 in) square, or a bit smaller. Return to the pan with the onion, 1–2 tablespoons of the oil and the garlic and fry for a couple of minutes. Season well.

2 Arrange the potatoes and onion down the centre of a large ovenproof dish. Scatter the tomatoes on top, and season again.

3 Put the peppers, cut side down, on to the grill rack and grill under the hot grill until the skin blisters and blackens. While the peppers are still hot, put into a polythene bag and seal the top so that they sweat. When cool enough to handle, peel off the skin and cut the flesh into quarters.

4 Mix the peppers with the olives, season and coat with olive oil. Spoon the peppers and olives down either side of the potatoes. Cover with foil.

Serves 6

TO PREPARE AHEAD

Prepare the vegetables ahead to the end of step 4. Keep in the fridge until needed (overnight if you like). Sear the skin of the fish for 1 minute, as in step 5. Transfer to a plate and chill until ready to cook (again, this could be done the night before). Keep the fish and vegetables separate. Reheat and cook as in steps 6 and 7. Not suitable for freezing.

TO COOK IN THE AGA

Char-grill the fish ahead, skin side down, in a ridged grill pan, on the Boiling Plate for about 1 minute, or until the skin is crisp and brown. About 30 minutes before serving, reheat the vegetables on the floor of the Roasting Oven for about 20 minutes. Lay the fish on top of the potatoes, skin side up, and roast at the top of the Roasting Oven for 8 minutes.

5 Slash the fish skin and brush with a little oil. Season the fish and fry, skin side down, in a very hot frying pan or ridged grill pan over high heat for about 1 minute, or until the skin is crisp and brown. The flesh will still be raw underneath.

6 Reheat the vegetables, covered, in the preheated oven for about 20 minutes, until very steamy and exceedingly hot. Remove the foil.

7 Lay the fish on top of the potatoes, skin side up, and return to the hot oven. Bake for about 8–10 minutes, or until just cooked. Sprinkle with parsley and basil to serve.

Monkfish Provençal with Crisp Bacon Lardons

These firm fish fillets, with their Mediterranean sauce, are very good served with rice and perhaps a green salad.

4 x 150g (5 oz) monkfish tail
  fillets, skinned
8 rashers smoked streaky bacon,
  snipped into thin strips
salt and freshly ground black
  pepper
1 tablespoon olive oil
2 tablespoons chopped fresh
  parsley

TOMATO HERB SAUCE
1 tablespoon olive oil

1 onion, chopped
2–3 garlic cloves, crushed
1 x 400g can chopped tomatoes
2 tablespoons sun-dried tomato
  paste
1 teaspoon chopped fresh
  tarragon
1 teaspoon balsamic vinegar
salt and freshly ground black
  pepper
1 teaspoon caster sugar, to taste

Preheat the oven to 200°C/Fan 180°C/Gas 6. You will need an ovenproof serving dish large enough to hold the fish in one layer.

1 First make the sauce. Heat the oil in a large frying pan, add the onion and garlic, and fry gently for 8 minutes, stirring from time to time until the onion is soft. Add the tomatoes, tomato paste, tarragon, vinegar, salt, pepper and sugar, and bring back to the boil. Turn into the serving dish.
2 Meanwhile, cook the snipped bacon in a frying pan for about 10 minutes until crisp, shaking from time to time. Set aside and keep warm (or, if preparing ahead, keep in the fridge).
3 Ensure all the stiff white membrane has been removed from the fish, then season well. Heat the oil in a frying pan and quickly fry the monkfish on all sides for about 3–4 minutes until golden brown, making sure it is not quite cooked through completely. Lay the tails on the tomato herb sauce.
4 Slide the serving dish into the preheated oven and cook, uncovered, for about 15 minutes, or until piping hot.
5 Remove from the oven, sprinkle with the warm crispy bacon and chopped parsley, and serve immediately.

Serves 4

TO PREPARE AHEAD
Prepare to the end of step 3 up to 6 hours ahead. Cover and keep in the fridge. Continue from step 4. Only the sauce is suitable for freezing. Freeze at the end of step 1 for up to a month.

TO COOK IN THE AGA
At step 1, make the sauce on the Boiling Plate in the usual way, then transfer to the floor of the Simmering Oven for 10 minutes for the onion to soften. For step 3, use the Boiling Plate. In step 4, cook on the grid shelf on the floor of the Roasting Oven for about 15 minutes, or until piping hot. If making the sauce ahead, reheat the bacon in the Simmering Oven for 5–10 minutes before adding at step 5.

TO PREPARE AHEAD
Prepare completely 24 hours in advance, and keep in the fridge. Not suitable for freezing.

TO COOK IN THE AGA
Slide the dish on to the grid shelf on the floor of the Roasting Oven and bake for about 25 minutes.

Triple Fish and Broccoli Bake

This dish is perfect for feeding the family or friends for supper. It can be made ahead of time, and simply popped into the hot oven to serve.

Crème fraîche can be bought as full fat or half fat. When heating for a sauce for pasta or any hot dish, it is important to use full fat as the half-fat version contains more water and goes very thin and runny. If using full-fat crème fraîche in hot dishes, it is reasonably thick once reduced a little. With half-fat crème fraîche, you will need to add a stabiliser such as cornflour, as in this recipe, otherwise it will be too runny. However, the half-fat version is perfect for cold dishes, or in a sauce to go with fish, mixed with fresh herbs.

225g (8 oz) broccoli
1 tablespoon cornflour
1 x 400ml carton half-fat crème fraîche
75g (3 oz) Parmesan, grated
2 teaspoons Dijon mustard
300g (10 oz) salmon fillets, skinned and sliced into 5cm (2 in) cubes

300g (10 oz) cod fillets, skinned and sliced into 5cm (2 in) cubes
75g (3 oz) shelled cooked prawns
salt and freshly ground black pepper
25g (1 oz) fresh breadcrumbs

Preheat the oven to 220°C/Fan 200°C/Gas 7. You will need a shallow ovenproof dish, with a capacity of about 1.7 litres (3 pints).

1 Trim the broccoli into small florets. Bring a pan of salted water up to a rolling boil. Add the broccoli florets and boil for about 3–4 minutes, then drain and refresh in cold water until cold. Dry well, and set aside.
2 In a large bowl, mix the cornflour with 3 tablespoons of the crème fraîche to combine, then add the rest of the crème fraîche, half the cheese and all the mustard. Fold in the salmon, cod, prawns and broccoli, and season well. Spoon into the ovenproof dish.
3 Sprinkle the top of the dish with breadcrumbs and the remaining cheese. Bake in the centre of the preheated oven for about 20–25 minutes, or until golden brown on top, bubbling around the edges and the fish is cooked.

Roasted Cod with Goat's Cheese and Sun-Dried Tomato

Use cod from a sustainable source, or substitute haddock fillet. I use soft goat's cheese that comes in a tub rather than the firmer roll. It is low fat too.

4 x 150g (5 oz) pieces of cod
  fillet, skinned
salt and freshly ground black
  pepper
4 tablespoons sun-dried tomato
  paste, from a jar or tube
1 x 150g carton soft goat's
  cheese

25g (1 oz) fresh white
  breadcrumbs
25g (1 oz) mature Cheddar,
  grated
a little paprika

Preheat the oven to 200°C/Fan 180°C/Gas 6.

1 Season the cod with a little salt and black pepper on both sides and arrange on a baking sheet.
2 Spread the sun-dried tomato paste evenly over the top of each cod fillet. Repeat with the goat's cheese.
3 Mix together the breadcrumbs and grated cheese, and press on top of the goat's cheese. Dust with a little paprika.
4 Bake in the preheated oven for about 12–15 minutes, or until the fish is white and no longer opaque, and golden brown on top.
5 Serve with new potatoes and green veg or Puy lentils.

Serves 4

TO PREPARE AHEAD

Prepare to the end of step 2 up to 24 hours ahead. Cover and keep in the fridge. Just before cooking, spread with the breadcrumbs and cheese. Not suitable for freezing.

TO COOK IN THE AGA

Slide the baking sheet on to the second set of runners in the Roasting Oven and cook for about 12 minutes.

TO PREPARE AHEAD

Once prepared up to the end of step 3, the dish can be kept in the fridge, covered, for up to 12 hours. Not suitable for freezing.

TO COOK IN THE AGA

At step 4, slide the ovenproof dish on to the grid shelf on the floor of the Roasting Oven and bake for about 20 minutes, or until the fish is just cooked.

Crusted Haddock Peperonata

This is a perfect recipe to prepare ahead as it is all cooked in one dish and popped in the oven at the last minute. Peperonata is an Italian mixture of red peppers, tomatoes, onions and garlic cooked in olive oil. For this recipe, I have added fennel too. This dish works just as well using other fresh white fish.

6 x 150g (5 oz) fresh haddock fillets, skinned
salt and freshly ground black pepper
6 dessertspoons tartare sauce, from a jar
about 50g (2 oz) coarse breadcrumbs (leftover ciabatta bread is ideal)
a little paprika
3 tablespoons chopped fresh parsley

1 very large onion, roughly chopped
2 Romano red peppers, halved lengthways, seeded and thickly sliced
1 large fresh fennel bulb, core removed and roughly chopped
2 garlic cloves, crushed
1 x 200g can chopped tomatoes
½ teaspoon caster sugar
2 tablespoons capers, drained and rinsed

PEPERONATA BASE
1–2 tablespoons olive oil

Preheat the oven to 200°C/Fan 180°C/Gas 6. You will need a shallow, fairly flat ovenproof dish large enough for the fish to sit in one layer.

1 First make the peperonata base. Heat the oil in a large non-stick frying pan. Add the onion and fry over a high heat for 2–3 minutes. Add the peppers, fennel, garlic and tomatoes, stirring well, and bring to the boil.

2 Season well, add the sugar, and continue to fry for about 10 minutes, stirring, to drive off any water, until the onions and fennel start to soften. Remove from the heat, stir in the capers and spoon into the ovenproof

dish. It is important to drive off any liquid which comes out of the vegetables before spooning into the dish; otherwise the sauce will be very wet and runny.

3 Season the fish on both sides and arrange on top of the vegetables. Spread about 1 dessertspoon of tartare sauce on each fillet, and sprinkle with the breadcrumbs. Season well and sprinkle with paprika.

4 Bake in the preheated oven for about 20 minutes, or until the fish is cooked and piping hot. Sprinkle with the chopped parsley and serve immediately.

Chicken and Poultry

I am a great fan of chicken as an ingredient – it is easy to cook and delicious to eat – and it is worth buying the best free-range chicken that you can afford. In fact, I almost consider chicken as one of the ultimate 'convenience' foods – it comes in such convenient portions of breasts, legs, wings and thighs. I have introduced many different flavours, using a number of bought ingredients – Thai sauces, shiitake mushrooms, etc. – but there are some old favourites as well, such as Coq au Vin.

The duck recipes include my adaptation of the classic French dish duck with orange. I'm pleased to see that duck is very much more available now in supermarkets, both whole and in portions – as indeed are pheasants and guinea fowl. Pheasant has always been a favourite of mine, but I do encourage you to try guinea fowl, which tastes like slightly gamey chicken.

If you have the time, make stock from any poultry or game bones. This is so useful to have in the freezer when frozen in clean cream cartons, ready to use in soups, sauces and gravies.

Many of the recipes can be prepared ahead to a certain extent, especially the stew-type dishes, which can be frozen up to a month in advance of when you want to serve them. That should guarantee a stress-free dinner-party main course – so long as you remember to defrost them in time!

For more poultry ideas, see:

Garlic-Stuffed Chicken with Thyme and Chives

Serves 6 as a hot main course, or 10 if serving cold as part of a buffet or picnic

Take care not to overcook the chicken, otherwise it will lose its moisture and flavour, and the bright green of the herbs will fade.

6 boned chicken breasts, skin left on
salt and freshly ground black pepper
butter, melted

STUFFING
heaped teaspoon of butter

1 medium onion, chopped
225g (8 oz) full-fat soft cheese
1 good tablespoon mixed chopped fresh chives and thyme
2 fat garlic cloves, crushed
1 large egg yolk
a little freshly grated nutmeg

Preheat the oven to 200°C/Fan 180°C/Gas 6. Butter and season a large roasting dish.

1 First make the stuffing. Melt the butter in a small pan and sauté the onion for 5 minutes. Cover and simmer for 10 minutes, or until tender.
2 Turn the onion into a bowl, allow to cool slightly, then mix with all the other stuffing ingredients. Mash down and season well.
3 Place the chicken breasts on a board, skin side uppermost. Loosen the skin from one side. Stuff a sixth of the cheese mixture into this pocket and replace the skin. Repeat the process with the remaining chicken breasts.
4 Arrange the chicken in the roasting tin and brush with melted butter. Roast in the preheated oven for about 20 minutes, or until just done.
5 Serve hot, warm or cold, slicing each breast into 3–4 diagonal slices to show off the stuffing. If serving hot, strain off any juices in the tin and make a good thin gravy, adding a little reduced white wine and cream if liked. If serving cold, allow the chicken to get cold before slicing.

TO PREPARE AHEAD

Complete to the end of step 3. Cover and keep in the fridge for up to 24 hours. Continue with step 4. Freezes well after step 3 for up to 2 months.

TO COOK IN THE AGA

For step 1, melt the butter and sauté the onion on the Simmering Plate, then cover and transfer to the Simmering Oven for 10 minutes to soften. At step 4, roast the chicken in the Roasting Oven, on the highest set of runners, for about 15 minutes, or until just done. If the chicken gets too brown, transfer to the floor of the Roasting Oven.

Braemar Pheasant

This recipe uses just the pheasant breasts, so keep the legs for a casserole or stock. Leeks and bacon go really well together in game recipes. If you can't get hold of bacon lardons, just cube thick slices of streaky bacon.

2 tablespoons sunflower oil
6 pheasant breasts, skinned
100g (4 oz) smoked bacon lardons
2 leeks, washed and coarsely shredded
25g (1 oz) flour
300ml (10 fl oz) apple juice
300ml (10 fl oz) chicken stock

1 tablespoon cranberry jelly or redcurrant jelly
2–3 sprigs fresh parsley
1 large sprig fresh thyme
1 bay leaf
salt and freshly ground black pepper
a generous amount of chopped fresh parsley

1 Heat a non-stick frying pan, add the oil and fry the pheasant breasts quickly over a high heat until browned on each side. Remove with a slotted spoon and set aside.

2 Add the bacon and the leeks to the same unwashed pan and cook until the leeks are beginning to brown and the bacon is crisp. If they become a little dry, add a little more oil. Add the flour to the pan and cook, stirring, for 1 minute. Gradually blend in the apple juice, stock and jelly. Bring to the boil, stirring until thickened.

3 Return the browned pheasant to the pan, add the herbs and seasoning, and bring to the boil. Cover and simmer gently for about 10–15 minutes, or until the pheasant is tender. Keep warm and rest for 15 minutes before serving.

4 Taste the sauce for seasoning, remove the bay leaf and thyme, and sprinkle over the parsley. Serve with mashed potato.

Serves 6

TO PREPARE AHEAD

Prepare to the end of step 3. Cool quickly, cover and keep in the fridge for up to 1 day. Reheat until piping hot to serve. Freeze at the end of step 3, for up to a month, but take care not to overcook the pheasant in the first place.

TO COOK IN THE AGA

Bring to the boil on the Boiling Plate, cover and transfer to the Simmering Oven and bake for about 10–15 minutes, or until the pheasant is tender. Allow to rest for 15 minutes before serving.

TO PREPARE AHEAD
Can be made completely and kept covered in the fridge up to 48 hours ahead. Not suitable for freezing.

TO COOK IN THE AGA
Bring up to the boil on the Boiling Plate, then transfer to the Simmering Oven for about 45 minutes, or until tender.

Thai Shiitake Chicken

Quite my most favourite Thai dish. Tamarind is the fruit of a leguminous, evergreen tree. The pulp, sold in jars, is used to add a distinctive flavour to chutneys and spicy dishes.

1 tablespoon sunflower oil
12 chicken thighs, skinless and
  boneless
1 large onion, thinly sliced
300g (10 oz) shiitake
  mushrooms, sliced
1–2 tablespoons red Thai curry
  paste
2 tablespoons tamarind paste
2 x 400ml can coconut milk

2 teaspoons fish sauce
juice and finely grated zest
  of 2 limes
2 teaspoons caster sugar
salt and freshly ground black
  pepper
2 tablespoons cornflour, slaked
  with a little coconut milk
chopped fresh basil or coriander

Preheat the oven to 160°C/Fan 140°C/Gas 3.

1 Heat the oil in a large non-stick frying pan or casserole dish. Brown the chicken thighs over a high heat until brown. Set aside. Add the onion and mushrooms to the pan and fry for 2–3 minutes.

2 Add the Thai paste, tamarind paste, coconut milk, fish sauce, lime juice and zest, and sugar. Bring to the boil and boil for 2–3 minutes. Season well.

3 Add a little hot sauce to the slaked cornflour and tip into the pan with the sauce, stirring continually while bringing it back to the boil. The sauce will thicken. Return the chicken thighs to the pan.

4 Cover the pan with a lid, transfer to the oven and bake for about 45 minutes or until the chicken is tender.

5 Sprinkle with the chopped coriander or basil, and serve hot.

The duck skin can be roasted ahead and reheated. Pre-fry the duck breasts (up to the end of step 2) and make the sauce (step 4). Roast the duck breasts from cold for 8 minutes, reheat the sauce and serve. Not suitable for freezing.

Brown the duck on the Boiling Plate. Roast on the grid shelf on the floor of the Roasting Oven for 6 minutes, or 8 minutes from cold. Rest before carving.

Roast Duck Breast with Sharp Mustard Sauce

I have always had difficulty in getting duck skin really crisp. I find the answer is to take the skins off with a sharp knife, lay them flat in a roasting tin and slow-roast at about 110°C/ Fan 90°C/Gas ¼ for about 4 hours (or in the Simmering Oven of the Aga) and keep checking until crisp. Drain off the fat – lovely for roast potatoes – then snip the skins into strips and serve with the duck.

4 duck breasts, skinned
2 tablespoons olive oil
salt and freshly ground black pepper
8 whole chives, to garnish

MARINADE
1 heaped teaspoon paprika
1 garlic clove, sliced
1 tablespoon olive oil

SHARP MUSTARD SAUCE
1 x 200ml carton full-fat crème fraîche
2 teaspoons grainy mustard
2 teaspoons lemon juice
1 teaspoon caster sugar
3 tablespoons snipped fresh chives

1 Prepare the marinade. In a large bowl, mix together the paprika, garlic and oil. Add the duck breasts and coat them in the marinade. Cover the bowl with clingfilm and leave to marinate in the fridge overnight or as long as possible.

Preheat the oven to 200°C/Fan 180°C/Gas 6. Grease a baking sheet.

2 Heat the oil in a large frying pan. Season the duck and brown the breasts for about 3 minutes on each side over a medium heat.
3 Transfer to the prepared baking sheet. Roast in the preheated oven for 8 minutes for medium pink in the middle, then rest for 5 minutes.
4 To make the sauce, add the crème fraîche to the unwashed frying pan and scrape up the bits from the bottom of the pan (if they have burnt, discard them) Add the mustard, lemon juice and sugar, and bring up to the boil. Season and add the snipped chives.
5 Once the duck has rested, carve each breast into 6 slices and arrange on plates. Spoon over the mustard sauce and serve at once, decorated with a cross of chives.

Mary Berry's Stress-free Kitchen

Coq au Vin

Back in the 1960s this was a great favourite, and now it is back in fashion, like many other classic French dishes. This recipe uses thighs rather than a traditional whole chicken as it saves carving the chicken before serving. I use ready-cut lardons of bacon for ease but you could also use the same amount of thick streaky bacon slices and cut them into small pieces. If time is really short, some supermarkets now sell ready peeled onions!

1 bottle red wine (about
 750ml/1½ pints)
25g (1 oz) butter
2 tablespoons olive oil
salt and freshly ground black
 pepper
12 chicken thighs, skinned and
 bone left in
225g (8 oz) smoked bacon
 lardons
20 whole baby onions, peeled
1 small head celery, cut into 1cm
 (½ in) slices
250g (9 oz) small button
 mushrooms, cleaned and left
 whole

1 large garlic clove, crushed
25g (1 oz) plain flour
1 tablespoon tomato purée
200ml (7 fl oz) chicken stock
3 sprigs fresh thyme
2 tablespoons redcurrant jelly

GARNISH (OPTIONAL)
100g (4 oz) smoked bacon
 lardons
225g (8 oz) small button
 mushrooms
a knob of butter
2 tablespoons chopped fresh
 parsley

Preheat the oven to 160°C/Fan 140°C/Gas 3.

1 Pour the wine into a large wide-based pan and boil over a high heat for about 10 minutes or until it has reduced to 425ml (15 fl oz). Set aside.

2 Melt half of the butter and all the oil in a large deep frying pan. Season the thighs, then brown in batches until golden. Remove with a slotted spoon and set aside. Fry the lardons in the same pan until crisp, then set aside.

3 Add the remaining butter to the pan and fry the onions, celery, mushrooms and garlic for 2–3 minutes. Sprinkle in the flour and stir to coat the vegetables. Pour the reduced wine, tomato purée and chicken

Serves 6–8

TO PREPARE AHEAD
At the end of step 3, cool, cover and keep in the fridge up to 2 days ahead. Reheat gently to serve with the garnish. Freeze the complete dish for up to 2 months.

TO COOK IN THE AGA
Brown the chicken on the Boiling Plate. Simmer the casserole in the Simmering Oven for 1–1½ hours, or until tender.

stock into the pan, and stir over the heat until boiling. Add the chicken, bacon lardons, sprigs of thyme, redcurrant jelly and some seasoning. Cover with a lid and simmer in the preheated oven for about 1 hour, or until the chicken is tender and the vegetables are soft.

4 When the chicken is almost cooked, make the garnish. In a dry non-stick pan, fry the lardons until crisp, then remove with a slotted spoon and set aside. Toss the mushrooms into the pan with a good knob of butter. Cook for 2–3 minutes over a high heat to drive off the moisture and brown the mushrooms. Return the lardons to the pan and heat through.

5 Remove the chicken from the oven, discarding the thyme sprigs. Add the parsley to the garnish and sprinkle over the chicken to serve.

Mustard-Crusted Chicken

Years ago we all enjoyed Wiener schnitzel. This is a similar, very fast supper dish, using chicken.

2 large chicken breasts, skinned
salt and freshly ground black
   pepper
about 50g (2 oz) dried
   breadcrumbs
about 3 tablespoons Dijon
   mustard

finely grated zest of 1 lemon
about 2 tablespoons sunflower
   or vegetable oil
4 eggs
1 small lemon, cut into wedges,
   to garnish

1 Carefully slice each chicken breast in half lengthways to give 2 thin breasts. Cover with clingfilm and beat with a rolling pin until each is very thin.

2 Season both sides of the chicken. Sprinkle the breadcrumbs on a plate. Spread one side of the chicken generously with mustard and press, mustard side down, into the crumbs. Spread the other side with mustard, sprinkle with lemon zest, then turn the chicken over in the crumbs. Now both sides are coated in mustard and crumbs.

3 Heat 1 tablespoon of the oil in a non-stick frying pan and pan-fry the chicken for about 1–2 minutes on each side, or until golden brown and cooked right through. Remove with a slotted spoon, drain on kitchen paper and keep hot.

4 In the same pan, heat the remaining oil and fry the eggs.

5 Top each chicken escalope with a fried egg. Serve immediately with the lemon wedges.

Serves 4

TO PREPARE AHEAD
Prepare to the end of step 2 up to 12 hours ahead. Cook to serve immediately, as it is so quick. Freeze at the end of step 2.

TO COOK IN THE AGA
Fry the chicken and eggs in a non-stick pan on the Boiling Plate.

TO PREPARE AHEAD

Can be made up to the end of step 4 but omitting the fresh mango. Keep covered in the fridge for up to 2 days. Continue with step 5, adding the fresh mango. Not suitable for freezing.

TO COOK IN THE AGA

Make the stock on the Boiling Plate. Once boiled, cover and transfer to Simmering Oven for about 2 hours. Make the sauce on the Boiling Plate. At step 5 slide the dish on to the second set of runners in the Roasting Oven and bake for about 15 minutes, or until brown on top and piping hot.

Highland Pheasant with a Touch of Mango

This is an excellent recipe for using up pheasants from the freezer when you are not too sure how long they've been there, or how old the birds are. It also produces plenty of delicious stock for use in other recipes. Remember to start the stock the day before.

a brace of pheasants
1 tablespoon vegetable oil
2 large onions, chopped
50g (2 oz) plain flour
1 x 250ml carton full-fat crème fraîche
4 good tablespoons mango chutney
3 tablespoons Worcestershire sauce
salt and freshly ground black pepper

1 small mango, peeled, and chopped or sliced
1 tablespoon chopped fresh parsley (use the stalks for the stock)

STOCK
2 sticks celery, each cut into three
1 carrot, cut in half
1 onion, quartered
1 bay leaf
2–3 parsley stalks

The stock can either be made on the hob or in the oven. If using the oven, preheat to 160°C/ Fan 140°C/Gas 3.

1 Make the stock the day before. Trim off the skin and any excess fat from the pheasants, and arrange snugly in a casserole or pan just large enough to hold them together with the stock ingredients and some seasoning. Cover with cold water, bring to the boil and simmer very gently for 1½–2 hours, or until the pheasants are very tender. If preferred, simmer in the preheated oven for about 1½–2 hours. Leave to cool completely in the liquid, as this will ensure that the pheasants are moist. Reserve 225ml (8 fl oz) stock and set aside.

2 When the pheasants are cool, carefully strip all the meat from the birds and cut into neat pieces, discarding all the bones and skin. Use the bones to enrich the leftover stock to use for another occasion.

Preheat the oven to 200°C/Fan 180°C/Gas 6.

3 Heat a largish non-stick frying pan, add the oil and the onions. Fry for a minute or two, cover, and cook over a medium heat for about 10 minutes, or until soft. Add the flour and stir. Blend in the measured stock, stirring well, and bring to the boil. Once thickened, stir in the crème fraîche.

4 Stir in the mango chutney and Worcestershire sauce, and season well. Add half the fresh mango and the strips of pheasant meat. If the sauce is a little thick, thin it down using more stock. Turn into an sided ovenproof dish that is not too shallow.

5 Reheat in the preheated oven for about 15 minutes, or until brown on top and piping hot.

6 Garnish with remaining fresh mango and the chopped parsley. Serve with mashed potato and a green salad or broccoli.

Tender Roasted Duck Legs with Orange and Ginger Sauce

Simmering the duck legs in stock makes them moist, and adding the ginger ensures they are full of flavour.

6 duck legs, trimmed of the last hock joint
1 chicken stock cube
1 x 2.5cm (1 in) piece fresh ginger root, peeled and cut into 3

MARINADE AND SAUCE
425ml (15 fl oz) orange juice, from a good-quality carton

2 garlic cloves, crushed
3 tablespoons dark soy sauce
1 x 1cm (½ in) piece fresh ginger root, peeled and grated
1 tablespoon fresh thyme leaves
1 level teaspoon cornflour
3 tablespoons cold water
salt and freshly ground black pepper

The first step can either be cooked on the hob or in the oven. If using the oven, preheat to 160°C/Fan 140°C/Gas 3.

1 Put the duck legs into a large saucepan, cover with cold water, and add the stock cube and pieces of ginger. Bring to the boil, cover and simmer gently for about 1½ hours, or until the duck is very tender. Alternatively, cook in a casserole in the preheated oven for the same amount of time.
2 Allow the duck to cool in the stock.
3 In a bowl big enough to hold the duck, mix together all the ingredients for the marinade, except for the cornflour, stirring well to combine.
4 Drain the duck legs from the stock (discarding the stock) and sit them in the marinade. Marinate for about 2 hours, or as long as possible.

Preheat the oven to 200°C/Fan 180°C/Gas 6. Line a baking sheet with non-stick baking paper.

5 Drain the duck, reserving the marinade. Arrange on the prepared baking sheet and roast near the top of the preheated oven for about 20–25 minutes, or until piping hot, crisp and brown.

6 Meanwhile, slake the cornflour with the cold water and pour into the marinade. Bring to the boil, stirring continuously until thickened. Check the seasoning.

7 Serve a little sauce with each crispy duck leg, and offer the remainder separately.

Guinea Fowl with Port and Blueberry Sauce

Serves 8

Traditionalists, like my husband Paul, prefer the sauce in the recipe without the blueberries! Blueberries go well with game and are very popular as a superfood right now. If you joint the guinea fowl ahead, you can use the carcass to make stock for the recipe.

Cook completely to the end of step 4, and keep in the fridge for about 12 hours. Continue, adding the blueberries when the guinea fowl is piping hot. Freeze at the end of step 4 for up to a month.

2 guinea fowl, about 1kg (2½ lb) each
salt and freshly ground black pepper
2 tablespoons olive oil
chopped fresh parsley

SAUCE
450ml (16 fl oz) guinea fowl stock or good chicken stock

3 tablespoons cornflour
100ml (4 fl oz) port
3 tablespoons redcurrant jelly
2 tablespoons soy sauce
1–2 tablespoons Worcestershire sauce
salt and freshly ground black pepper
225g (8 oz) fresh blueberries

TO COOK IN THE AGA

Use the Boiling Plate for steps 1–3. At step 4, cook in the Simmering Oven for about 30 minutes, or until tender. Make the stock, bring to the boil on the Boiling Plate, cover and transfer to Simmering Oven for about 2 hours. Freezes well but add the blueberries when reheating.

This recipe can either be cooked on the hob or in the oven. If using the oven, preheat to 160°C/Fan 140°C/Gas 3.

1 Take off the thigh/leg joints and the breast/wing joints from the guinea fowl, making 8 joints from the two birds. Trim off all excess fat and season well. (To make stock from the carcass and backbones, put the bones in your smallest pan, cover with water and add vegetables to flavour. Simmer for 2 hours, then strain the stock.)

2 Fry the guinea fowl joints in the oil on both sides in a large non-stick frying pan over a high heat until golden brown all over. Remove from the pan and set aside, draining off any fat. Wipe out the frying pan with kitchen paper.

3 Make the sauce by blending 4 tablespoons of stock with the cornflour in a bowl. Measure into the wiped frying pan the port, remaining stock, redcurrant jelly, soy sauce, Worcestershire sauce and seasoning. Whisk in the blended cornflour mixture and bring to the boil, stirring and allowing it to thicken.

4 Return the browned joints to the frying pan with the sauce. Bring to the boil again, cover and simmer very gently for about 30 minutes, or until tender. Alternatively, cook in the preheated oven for 30 minutes, or until tender.

5 In the last 2–3 minutes of cooking time, add the blueberries to the pan. Serve sprinkled with the parsley. Good with mashed potatoes.

Devilled Chicken

This recipe couldn't be easier, and it's very popular with the young – ideal, in fact, for a family supper.

12 chicken thighs, skinless and
  boneless
salt and freshly ground black
  pepper

SAUCE
1 rounded tablespoon apricot
  jam
1 teaspoon Dijon mustard

a good pinch cayenne pepper
1 large garlic clove, crushed
1 tablespoon Worcestershire
  sauce
3 tablespoons tomato ketchup
1 tablespoon dark soy sauce

Preheat the oven to 190°C/Fan 170°C/Gas 5. Grease and well season a roasting tin.

1 Season the chicken thighs well on all sides and put in the roasting tin.
2 Measure the jam into a bowl, add the mustard, cayenne, garlic and Worcestershire sauce, and blend well until smooth. Add the other ingredients, season lightly, not adding too much salt, and pour over the chicken, coating evenly.
3 Bake in the preheated oven for about 20–30 minutes, or until cooked through and golden brown. Turn halfway through cooking. To test when the chicken is done, prod the thickest part with a fine skewer. If the juices run out clear, the chicken is done; if pink, give the chicken a little longer.
4 Serve hot with rice and a green salad.

Serves 6

TO PREPARE AHEAD
Complete to the end of step 2. Cover and refrigerate for about 8 hours. Freezes well at the end of step 2 for up to 2 months.

TO COOK IN THE AGA
At step 3, slide the roasting tin on to the top set of runners in the Roasting Oven and cook for about 15 minutes, or until golden brown.

Chicken Olives Provençal

This is a super family supper dish. Boneless chicken thighs are readily available from all good supermarkets. The stuffing and sauce are very easy to do and the chicken doesn't need browning ahead.

TO PREPARE AHEAD

Complete to the end of step 3, cover and keep in the fridge for up to 12 hours. The raw stuffed chicken thighs freeze very successfully at the end of step 2, for up to 2 months.

TO COOK IN THE AGA

For step 4, slide the dish on to the second set of runners in the Roasting Oven and bake for about 25–30 minutes, or until the chicken is tender and the sauce boiling.

3 large good-quality pork sausages
25g (1 oz) black olives, stoned and finely chopped
finely grated zest of 1 lemon
1 tablespoon finely chopped fresh thyme
1 tablespoon finely chopped fresh sage
salt and freshly ground black pepper
8 chicken thighs, skinless and boneless

25g (1 oz) Parmesan, coarsely grated
chopped fresh parsley, to garnish

SAUCE
2 tablespoons dark soy sauce
1 scant tablespoon Worcestershire sauce
1 tablespoon runny honey
2 teaspoons grainy mustard
1 x 400g can chopped tomatoes

Preheat the oven to 190°C/Fan 170°C/Gas 5. You will need an ovenproof dish about 28 x 23cm (11 x 9 in).

1 Slit each sausage skin lengthways and remove the meat, discarding the skins. Put the sausagemeat into a bowl, add the olives, lemon zest, thyme and sage. Season, and mix well.

2 Unfold and lay out the chicken thighs (smooth side down). Season well and fill with 1 tablespoon of the sausagemeat stuffing (where the bone would have been). Fold the sides towards the middle, over the stuffing. Arrange in the dish, join side down, and season the thighs all over.

3 In a bowl, blend together the sauce ingredients and pour over the thighs, ensuring all are covered. Sprinkle with the Parmesan.

4 Cook in the preheated oven for about 30–40 minutes, or until the chicken is tender and the sauce is piping hot.

5 Garnish with the parsley and serve with herby mashed potatoes.

Meat

The idea of cooking meat stresses many people, but it's all really a matter of understanding what the cuts of meat are, choosing carefully which ones you buy, and knowing how they ought to be cooked. The prime cuts of meat, such as fillet steak, are more expensive, and may be cooked briefly and fast; the cheaper cuts of meat are not necessarily lesser in quality, or indeed taste; they just need to be cooked for much longer. To help you on your way, get to know your local butcher, who will have been working with meat since his teens; he will be a fount of information and will relieve you of much of the stress of cutting, filleting, skinning and boning, if you ask him nicely.

There are lots of ideas here from around the world – Thai, French, Italian, Greek, Moroccan, etc. – some of which would make good supper or lunch dishes, while a few would be perfect for that special occasion, be it a kitchen supper or a smart party. Many of the dishes can be prepared well in advance, and, in fact, meat casseroles must be the most stress-free of dishes: after minimal preparation well in advance, you cook them slowly (while you concentrate on something else), and then you can often leave them to sit overnight in the fridge, for some casseroles are actually *better* a day or two after cooking.

For more meat ideas, see:

Burlington Beef

A tasty beef casserole, good enough for a supper party. The stir-fried garnish gives a lovely crunch to the dish. Serve with creamy mashed potato.

25g (1 oz) dried porcini
  mushrooms
450ml (15 fl oz) beef stock, hot
2 tablespoons sunflower oil
1kg (2¼ lb) good-quality
  braising steak, diced
2 tablespoons plain flour
150ml (5 fl oz) dry white wine
350g (12 oz) onions, thinly sliced
4 sticks celery, strings removed
  and diagonally sliced
3 garlic cloves, crushed
2 tablespoons apricot jam
1 sprig fresh thyme
salt and freshly ground black
  pepper

½ yellow pepper, seeded and
  thinly sliced
1 tablespoon balsamic vinegar
2 tablespoons chopped fresh
  flat-leaf parsley

GARNISH
1 tablespoon olive oil
½ yellow pepper, seeded and
  cut into julienne strips
175g (6 oz) chestnut mushrooms,
  thinly sliced
6 sprigs fresh flat-leaf parsley

Preheat the oven to 160°C/Fan 140°C/Gas 3.

1 Wash the dried mushrooms and soak in the hot stock for 20–30 minutes. Drain, reserving the soaking liquid. Slice the mushrooms into large pieces.

2 Heat the oil in a large pan and brown the beef in batches, then remove from the pan and set aside. Add the flour to the pan and stir to blend. Blend in the white wine, dried mushrooms and soaking liquid. Add the onion, celery and garlic, and cook for 5–6 minutes, stirring from time to time.

3 Return the meat to the pan, bring to the boil and simmer for 2–3 minutes. Stir in the apricot jam and thyme, and season well.

4 Cover the pan and transfer to the preheated oven. Cook for approximately 2½ hours, or until tender.

Serves 6

TO PREPARE AHEAD

Make the dish to the end of step 5 but add the balsamic vinegar. Cool, cover and keep in the fridge for up to 48 hours. To serve, stir-fry the garnish vegetables and add to the reheated casserole. Freeze at the end of step 5, for up to 2 months.

TO COOK IN THE AGA

For step 2, use the Boiling Plate to brown the beef. Slide the pan on to the Simmering Plate to blend in the flour and to complete step 3. At step 4, transfer to the floor of the Simmering Oven and cook for approximately 2½ hours, or until tender. To reheat after freezing, bring up to the boil in an ovenproof casserole on the Boiling Plate, stir, then transfer to the Roasting Oven on the second set of runners, and reheat for about 20 minutes. Stir-fry the garnish vegetables, and complete the dish.

5 About 20 minutes before the end of the cooking time, add the yellow pepper.

6 When nearly ready to serve, make the garnish. Heat the olive oil in a pan and stir-fry the pepper and mushrooms.

7 Remove the casserole from the oven, and add the balsamic vinegar and chopped parsley. Stir well and spoon on to warmed plates. Top each with 1 heaped spoonful of the garnish vegetables and a sprig of parsley.

Beef Florentine with Three Cheeses

This well-flavoured beef dish is topped with spinach and cheese, then finished with a layer of crisp filo pastry. It is easy and delicious. It was first given to me in Scotland as the lunch for the audience of one of my cookery demonstrations. Halve the quantities for 6 people.

SAVOURY BEEF LAYER
a good knob of butter
1.8kg (4 lb) good-quality lean minced beef
3 level tablespoons plain flour
2 x 400g cans chopped tomatoes
4 fat garlic cloves, crushed
4 good tablespoons tomato purée
1 generous teaspoon caster sugar
salt and freshly ground black pepper

SPINACH AND CHEESE LAYER
450g (1 lb) frozen leaf spinach, thawed
175g (6 oz) mature Cheddar, grated
175g (6 oz) Gruyère or Emmental cheese, grated
225g (8 oz) full-fat cream cheese
4 large eggs, beaten

TOPPING
about 17 sheets filo pastry
melted butter, for brushing

Preheat the oven to 200°C/ Fan 180°C/Gas 6. You will need a large ovenproof lasagne-type dish about 36 x 30cm (14 x 12 in).

1 First cook the minced beef. Melt the butter in a large pan, add the meat and cook for a couple of minutes over a high heat, stirring. When the natural fat begins to run out, brown the meat, stirring. Add the flour, mix well, then add the tomatoes, garlic, tomato purée, sugar and seasoning. Bring to the boil and simmer for 5 minutes. Then cover and simmer for 45 minutes, or until tender. Check the seasoning.

2 Next prepare the spinach filling. Squeeze all of the water out of the spinach. Turn into a bowl with the cheeses, then add the eggs. Season and mix well.

3 Spread half of the beef mixture in the dish. Top with the spinach mixture, then with a layer of the remaining beef.

Serves 12

TO PREPARE AHEAD
Prepare to the end of step 3. and keep in the fridge for up to 24 hours. Continue with step 4. Freeze at the end of step 3 for up to 1 month.

TO COOK IN THE AGA
At step 1, use the Simmering Plate to cook the meat. When the fat runs out, transfer to the Boiling Plate to brown the meat. Cover and simmer in the Simmering Oven. At step 5, bake on the grid shelf on the floor of the Roasting Oven for about 30–35 minutes, or until golden brown and bubbling at the edges.

4 Spread about 5 sheets of the filo pastry out on a table. Brush with melted butter. Cover the surface of the beef with 5 buttered sheets of filo, overlapping to fit the dish. Brush the remaining 12 sheets with melted butter. Scrunch up each sheet and arrange on top of the layered filo. This means that each person gets a crispy piece of scrunched filo, and the dish is easier to cut into portions.

5 Bake in the preheated oven for about 30–35 minutes, or until golden brown and bubbling at the edges.

Cumberland Crusted Lamb

A perfect way to use up the last of the Christmas walnuts that have sat around in the fruit bowl. This recipe is easy to prepare, with an equally quick and simple sauce.

2 trimmed French-style racks of lamb, the chop bones cut short, chine removed (usually 7 in each rack, 14 in total
a little beaten egg

CRUST MIXTURE
2 fat garlic cloves, quartered
a generous bunch fresh parsley, about 25g (1 oz), washed
1 slice wholemeal bread
2 tablespoons shelled walnut pieces
grated zest of 1 small lemon

1 tablespoon walnut oil (optional)
salt and freshly ground black pepper

SAUCE
1 heaped tablespoon flour
300ml (10 fl oz) white wine
150ml (5 fl oz) good beef stock
grated zest and juice of 1 lemon
grated zest and juice of 1 orange
4 tablespoons redcurrant jelly
a little gravy browning (optional)

Preheat the oven to 220°C/Fan 200°C/Gas 7.

1 Trim any surplus fat from the lamb and weigh, making a note of the weight. Paint the outer fat surface with a little beaten egg and reserve the rest for the crust.

2 Make the crust mixture. In a processor, using the metal blade, process the garlic briefly, then add the parsley and briefly process again. Add the bread and process to the count of 10. Add the walnuts, lemon zest and walnut oil (if using) and process to the count of 15. Add seasoning and the remaining egg, and whizz to combine. If you do not have a processor, chop the ingredients very finely and mix together in a bowl.

3 Divide the crust mixture in half and spread evenly over the outside of each rack of lamb. If time allows, prepare this ahead and chill for 30 minutes, as this helps to hold the crust.

4 Place the racks in a small roasting tin, bone ends towards the centre, and roast in the preheated oven for 25 minutes, or, for very pink, 15 minutes.

Serves 6

TO PREPARE AHEAD
Prepare the lamb to the end of step 3 up to 12 hours ahead. Roast in the preheated oven for about 15 minutes for rare, 25 minutes for well done. Not suitable for freezing.

TO COOK IN THE AGA
At step 4, place the racks in the small roasting tin and roast on the second set of runners in the Roasting Oven for 25 minutes, or, for very pink, 15 minutes. At step 6, make the sauce on the Simmering Plate, then slide the tin on to the floor of the Roasting Oven for 5 minutes to complete the cooking.

5 When the lamb is cooked, put it on a serving dish to keep warm while making the sauce.

6 For the sauce, add the flour to the roasting juices in the tin and scrape up all the bits, using a whisk if necessary. Add the wine, stock, the zests and juices, and the redcurrant jelly, and whisk again. Put the tin on the hob and cook for 5 minutes, whisking once. Taste for seasoning, and sieve. Add a little gravy browning if liked. Serve alongside the lamb.

Moussaka at its Best

A quick, modern moussaka. There is no frying of the aubergine slices first, as blanching is more healthy. Nor is there a classic white sauce to make; instead, the recipe uses Greek yoghurt and crème fraîche with a stabiliser of cornflour.

a little sunflower oil
900g (2 lb) raw minced lamb
2 large onions, roughly chopped
2 fat garlic cloves, crushed
2 level tablespoons flour
2 x 400g cans chopped tomatoes
4 tablespoons tomato purée
salt and freshly ground black
  pepper
3 large aubergines, cut into
  1½cm (¾ in) slices

TOPPING
2 level tablespoons cornflour
1 x 200ml carton Greek yoghurt
1 x 200ml carton full-fat crème
  fraîche
2 teaspoons Dijon mustard
75g (3 oz) Parmesan, grated

Preheat the oven to 200°C/Fan 180°C/Gas 6. You will need a large ovenproof dish about 34 x 24.5cm (13¼ x 9½ in).

1 Heat a large non-stick frying pan, add the oil and the mince and, using a wooden spoon, break up the lamb as it browns (you may need to do this in batches).
2 Return all the mince to the pan. Add the onions and cook over a high heat for 2–3 minutes. Add the garlic and blend in the flour. Add the tomatoes, tomato purée and seasoning, and stir well. Bring to the boil, allow to thicken, then cover and simmer over a low heat for about 45 minutes, or until the meat is tender.
3 Meanwhile, blanch the aubergines in boiling salted water for about 5 minutes, or until just tender. Drain, first in a colander and then on kitchen paper.
4 Make the topping. Measure the cornflour into a bowl, blend in a little yoghurt and whisk with a hand whisk until smooth. Mix in the remaining yoghurt, crème fraîche and mustard.

TO PREPARE AHEAD
This can be made completely and kept in the fridge for up to 2 days. Freeze at the end of step 6 for up to 2 months.

TO COOK IN THE AGA
After step 2, bring to the boil on the Boiling Plate. Then cover and transfer to the Simmering Oven to cook for about 1–2 hours. At step 6, cook the complete dish on the second set of runners in the Roasting Oven for about 45 minutes, or until golden brown and bubbling.

5 To assemble the moussaka, spread half the meat mixture over the bottom of the ovenproof dish. Cover with the aubergines, season well and spread with the remaining meat. Spread the topping over the lamb and sprinkle with the Parmesan.

6 Cook in the preheated oven for about 45 minutes, or until the top is brown and bubbling. Serve with a dressed green salad.

Tagine of Lamb

A traditional Moroccan dish, which is best made a day ahead and reheated.

1 tablespoon sunflower oil

900g (2 lb) neck fillet of lamb or lean boneless leg or shoulder of lamb, cut into 2.5cm (1 in) pieces

2 large onions, coarsely chopped

3 fat garlic cloves, crushed

175g (6 oz) ready-to-eat dried apricots, quartered

1 teaspoon ground ginger

1 teaspoon ground cinnamon

1 tablespoon paprika

¼ teaspoon hot chilli powder

a generous pinch of saffron, soaked in 3 tablespoons hot water

2 tablespoons honey

1 x 800g can chopped tomatoes

salt and freshly ground black pepper

chopped fresh parsley, to garnish

Preheat the oven to 160°C/Fan 140°C/Gas 3.

1 Heat the oil in a large frying pan and brown the lamb in batches. When brown, remove with a slotted spoon and set aside.

2 Add the onions and garlic to the unwashed pan, stir, then cover and cook over a gentle heat for about 10–15 minutes, or until soft.

3 Increase the heat and add the apricots, the spices, including the saffron and its soaking liquid, the honey and the tomatoes. Return the browned lamb to the pan. Bring to the boil. Season, cover and transfer to the preheated oven. Cook for about 2 hours, or until the meat is very tender. Check the seasoning.

4 Garnish with the parsley and serve with couscous and vegetables.

Serves 6–8

TO PREPARE AHEAD
Complete to the end of step 3 a day ahead. Freeze at the end of step 3 for up to 3 months.

TO COOK IN THE AGA
Sear the lamb on the Boiling Plate. Cook the onions in the Simmering Oven, covered, for 20 minutes. Cook the lamb to the end of step 3 in the Simmering Oven. Check from time to time, returning to the Boiling Plate if it is not cooking. Test whether the meat is tender after about 2 hours, depending on the temperature of your Simmering Oven.

Serves 4

TO PREPARE AHEAD

Make up to the end of step 3, and keep in the fridge for up to 2 days. Freeze at the end of step 3 for up to 2 months.

TO COOK IN THE AGA

At step 3, bring to the boil, cover and transfer to the Simmering Oven. Cook for about 15 minutes. Add the pork and return to the same oven for a further 10 minutes, or until the pork is tender.

Pork Mimosa

The wonderful blend of spices gives a real mellowness to this sauce, which is in no way hot and fiery. Serve with plain boiled rice and Raita (see below), mango chutney and fresh mango cut into cubes.
Coconut cream can be bought in cartons and is thick like single cream. If you can only buy coconut milk, use a 400g can.

25g (1 oz) butter
900g (2 lb) pork fillet, cut into 1cm (½ in) strips
1 large onion, cut into small wedges
2 fat garlic cloves, crushed
about 5cm (2 in) piece fresh ginger root, peeled and finely grated

1 level tablespoon each cumin, ground coriander, turmeric and medium curry powder
1 x 400g can chopped tomatoes
150ml (5 fl oz) chicken stock
1 x 200ml carton coconut cream
salt and freshly ground black pepper
fresh coriander or mint leaves, to garnish

1 Melt the butter in a fairly large saucepan over a high heat and brown the pork strips (you may need to do this in batches). Remove from the pan, using a slotted spoon, and set aside.

2 Add the onion and garlic to the unwashed pan and fry over a high heat for 2–3 minutes.

3 Add the ginger and spices, mix well and fry for 1 minute over a high heat. Add the tomatoes, stock and coconut cream, and stir until combined. Season, cover and simmer for about 15 minutes, or until the onion is tender. Return the pork to the pan and cook for a further 10 minutes, or until the pork is tender.

4 Spoon into a serving dish and decorate with the coriander or mint leaves. Serve hot with rice and raita.

Raita

A wonderful fresh accompaniment for any curry-flavoured dish.

1 x 7.5cm (3 in) piece cucumber,
  seeded and finely diced
salt and freshly ground black
  pepper

1 x 150ml carton plain yoghurt
about 6 sprigs fresh mint, leaves
  only, chopped

1 Sprinkle the prepared cucumber with salt and leave for about
30 minutes in a sieve. This extracts any liquid from the cucumber.
Drain off the liquid and pat the cucumber dry with kitchen paper.
2 Add the yoghurt and fresh mint, and season lightly. Stir and spoon
into a serving bowl. Serve chilled.

Foolproof Rice

*A foolproof way of cooking rice, using the absorption method. (If
you have an Aga, you can cook it in the Simmering Oven.) If you
are exact with quantities, every grain of rice will be separate.
Wild rice is the edible seed of a grass. I always cook it for the same
time as normal rice; if cooked for longer, it becomes mushy.*

300g (10 oz) easy-cook rice
  (e.g. Uncle Ben's)
50g (2 oz) wild rice (optional)
1 teaspoon salt

1 Measure the rice and wild rice (if using) into a saucepan. Add 450ml
(15 fl oz) water and the salt. Bring to the boil, cover and simmer over
a medium heat for about 15 minutes, or until all the liquid has been
absorbed and the rice is tender.

Serves 4

TO PREPARE AHEAD

**Can be made up to 2 days
ahead and kept covered in
the fridge. Not suitable for
freezing.**

Serves 4–6

TO COOK AND PREPARE AHEAD

**This method of cooking rice
is very quick and easy to do
so ideally cook and serve. If
you wish to reheat, it must
be cooked and cooled quickly
and kept covered in the
fridge for up to 24 hours. To
reheat, spoon into a buttered
ovenproof dish, cover with
foil and reheat at 200°C/Fan
180°C/Gas 6 for about 20
minutes until piping hot.
Not suitable for freezing.**

TO COOK IN THE AGA

**Bring to the boil, cover and
transfer to the Simmering
Oven. Cook for 15–20
minutes, or until all the liquid
has been absorbed and the
rice is tender.**

TO PREPARE AHEAD

At the end of step 4, store in the fridge for up to 2 days. Freeze at the end of step 4 for up to 3 months.

TO COOK IN THE AGA

Cover and reheat in the Roasting Oven for about 15 minutes, or until boiling. Remove the lid and cook for a further 5 minutes.

Baked Sausages with Double Onion Marmalade

This method of cooking sausages keeps them wonderfully succulent. Choose good-quality butcher's sausages – we like Pork and Leek.

1 tablespoon sunflower oil
25g (1 oz) butter
900g (2 lb) good-quality
   sausages
450g (1 lb) large red onions,
   thinly sliced
450g (1 lb) large white onions,
   thinly sliced

225ml (8 fl oz) red wine
50ml (2 fl oz) white wine vinegar
2 tablespoons sugar
salt and freshly ground black
   pepper
3 tablespoons chopped fresh
   parsley

Preheat the oven to 200°C/Fan 180°C/Gas 6.

1 Heat the oil and butter over a high heat in a large ovenproof pan and brown the sausages evenly. You may need to do this in batches. Remove the sausages with a slotted spoon and drain on kitchen paper. Set aside.

2 Pour off the excess fat to leave about 2 tablespoons in the pan. Add the onions and cook gently, stirring occasionally, for 10–15 minutes, or until soft.

3 Add the wine, vinegar, sugar and seasoning. Bring to the boil and allow to bubble for 2–3 minutes. Remove from the heat.

4 Arrange the sausages in a single layer on top of the onions and cook, uncovered, in the preheated oven, stirring occasionally, for about 45 minutes, or until the onions are meltingly soft.

5 Scatter with the parsley and serve with mashed potatoes.

Thai Burgers with Coriander Dipping Sauce

This is a wonderful way with burgers – great for a different summer barbecue – but don't overcook them.

450g (1 lb) best minced steak
3 spring onions, thinly sliced
1 teaspoon ground coriander
3 teaspoons red Thai curry paste
salt and freshly ground black
  pepper
olive or sunflower oil

2 tablespoons Thai dipping
  sauce, from a bottle
1 tablespoon chopped fresh
  coriander
salt and freshly ground black
  pepper

DIPPING SAUCE
1 x 250ml carton full-fat crème
  fraîche

1 In a large mixing bowl, use your hands to mix together the steak, spring onions, coriander, curry paste and seasoning, making sure all the spices are evenly distributed.

2 Wet your hands and shape the mix into 6 even-sized flat cakes.

3 Mix together the ingredients for the dipping sauce, and season well.

4 Preheat a ridged grill pan or non-stick frying pan over a high heat. Brush each side of the burgers with oil and fry for about 2½–3½ minutes on each side. Remove from the pan as soon as they are cooked right through (this depends on the thickness of each burger) and keep warm. To check whether they are done, split one and have a look: the meat should be brown and not pink.

5 Serve the hot burgers with the dipping sauce.

Serves 6

TO PREPARE AHEAD
At the end of step 2 the raw burgers can be kept covered in the fridge for 12 hours. Freeze at the end of step 2, for up to 1 month.

TO COOK IN THE AGA
At step 4, fry on the Boiling Plate.

French-Style Rack of Lamb with Proper Gravy

Rack of lamb is a roast for a special occasion. You may need to order it from your butcher in advance.

2 fully trimmed French-style
  racks of lamb, chine bone
  removed (usually 14 cutlets
  in total, 7 in each rack)
olive oil
salt and freshly ground black
  pepper

GRAVY
1 level tablespoon plain flour
65ml (2¼ fl oz) red wine
300ml (10 fl oz) chicken stock
1 teaspoon Worcestershire sauce
1 teaspoon lemon juice
1 tablespoon redcurrant jelly
a dash of gravy browning

Preheat the oven to 220°C/Fan 200°C/Gas 7.

1 Weigh the lamb and make a note of the weight. Rub with a little olive oil and season well.

2 In a non-stick frying pan, quickly brown the racks on the fatty side; a little colour makes them look more appetising.

3 Sit the racks in a small roasting tin, the bone tips facing downwards and inwards. Roast in the preheated oven: 12–15 minutes for pink lamb, 20 minutes for well done. The cooking time will depend on the thickness of the racks of lamb and how well they have been trimmed.

4 Remove the racks from the tin, wrap loosely in foil, and allow to rest for about 10 minutes while you make the gravy.

5 With the roasting tin off the heat, use a metal whisk to blend in the flour with the fat and meat juices. Pour in the wine and remaining ingredients, whisking well, and cook on the hob over a medium heat for about 5 minutes, or until bubbling and slightly thickened. Check the seasoning.

6 Serve 2–3 cutlets per person with the gravy, with potato cakes, stir-fried young spinach and young carrots.

Serves 4–6

TO PREPARE AHEAD
The red wine, Worcestershire sauce, lemon juice and redcurrant jelly can all be added to the stock ready to make the gravy at step 5. Not suitable for freezing.

TO COOK IN THE AGA
At step 3, roast the racks in the Roasting Oven towards the top for about 15 minutes.

TO PREPARE AHEAD
Make the sauce ahead up to the end of step 1, and keep in the fridge for up to 3 days. Freeze at the end of step 1 for up to 2 months.

TO COOK IN THE AGA
For step 1, fry the sausagemeat on the Boiling Plate. After adding the sauce ingredients, cover and transfer to the Simmering Oven to cook for about 30–40 minutes. If reheating the sauce after freezing, cook on the Simmering Plate while the pasta is cooking.

Pasta Milano

This pasta dish, with fusilli (corkscrew or spiral shapes), is not only inexpensive but a real winner for flavour. Rather than use plain pork sausagemeat, which I find far too fatty, I buy good pork sausages, preferably the true Luganega Italian sausages, or alternatively Waitrose Gourmet sausages.

Take care when chopping the chilli: wash your hands straight afterwards and do not put your hands near your eyes. If in doubt, chop with a knife and fork or wear rubber gloves.

350g (12 oz) dried fusilli
salt and freshly ground black
  pepper
50g (2 oz) Parmesan, coarsely
  grated
a small bunch chopped fresh
  basil
3 tablespoons chopped fresh
  parsley

1 tablespoon olive oil
3 garlic cloves, crushed
1 red chilli, seeded and finely
  chopped
2 x 400g cans chopped tomatoes
3 good tablespoons tomato
  purée
1 teaspoon caster sugar

SAUCE
350g (12 oz) best butcher's very
  lean, high-meat content, pork
  sausages

1 First make the sauce. Make long slits in each sausage and remove the meat. Discard the skins. Measure a little oil into a non-stick frying pan, and fry the sausagemeat over a high heat. Mash down and brown well, then stir in the remaining sauce ingredients. Bring to the boil, cover and simmer for 30–40 minutes or until the meat is tender and cooked. Check the seasoning.
2 Meanwhile, add the pasta to a large pan of boiling salted water. Bring back to the boil, then cover and cook until al dente, about 12 minutes. Drain and set aside.
3 Toss the sauce with the drained pasta, adding half the cheese and all the basil. Scatter the parsley and remaining Parmesan over individual portions.

Fillet Steak with Savoy Cabbage Potato Cakes

This very special fillet steak is served on a sort of bubble and squeak potato cake with a rich creamy horseradish sauce.

This recipe is designed to be part-cooked ahead of time, with the potato cakes and steaks being reheated just before serving, which makes it perfect for a dinner party. If, however, you want to cook and serve immediately, fry the potato cakes for a little longer and rest the steaks after frying for 5 minutes. Serve assembled with the sauce.

4 x 100–150g (4–5 oz) thick fillet
  steaks, cut from the centre of
  the fillet
25g (1 oz) butter, at room
  temperature
8 whole chive stems

SAVOY CABBAGE POTATO
CAKES
450g (1 lb) King Edward
  potatoes, peeled and cut into
  large cubes
½ small Savoy cabbage, thick
  core removed, leaves thinly
  sliced
3 tablespoons chopped fresh
  chives

1 large egg yolk
2 tablespoons milk
salt and freshly ground black
  pepper
a little sunflower oil, for frying

RICH AND SPECIAL
HORSERADISH SAUCE
a little butter
4 shallots, very finely chopped
2 garlic cloves, crushed
50ml (2 fl oz) medium sherry
100ml (4 fl oz) good beef stock
1 x 200ml carton full-fat crème
  fraîche
2 good tablespoons creamed
  horseradish sauce, from a jar

Serves 4

TO PREPARE AHEAD

Complete to the end of step 5 up to 24 hours ahead and keep in the fridge. Add any juices from cooking the steaks in step 6 to the sauce. The sauce, too, can be made up to 24 hours ahead. Not suitable for freezing.

TO COOK IN THE AGA

Fry the potato cakes and steaks as above in a hot pan on the Boiling Plate. At step 6, reheat the potato cake and steaks in the centre of the Roasting Oven.

1 First make the potato cakes. Put the potatoes into a saucepan, cover with salted water, bring to the boil and cook for about 10 minutes. Add the cabbage and continue to cook for another 5 minutes, or until the potatoes are soft. Drain and mash. Combine the chives, egg yolk and milk, add to the potato, and mix together with some seasoning.
2 Shape into 4 round cakes and put into the fridge to firm up for at least 1 hour.
3 Heat the oil in a large non-stick frying pan and brown the potato cakes for 2–3 minutes on each side until golden brown. Arrange at one end of a baking sheet.

4 Use your hand to flatten the steaks a little to a thickness of about 2cm (¾ in). Spread each side with butter and season well. Fry in the same frying pan as the potato cakes for 1½ minutes on each side. Remove and set aside.

5 To make the sauce, melt a little butter in a saucepan, add the shallots and garlic, and fry for 2–3 minutes, or until just pale golden. Take care not to let it get too dark. Add the sherry and stock, and boil over a high heat until reduced by half. Add the crème fraîche, horseradish, and some seasoning. It should be a thin pouring sauce. Set aside until needed.

Preheat the oven to 220°C/Fan 200°C/Gas 7.

6 To reheat, cook the potato cakes in the preheated oven for about 7 minutes, then add the steaks to the baking sheet and cook for a further 7 minutes.

7 Lay 1 potato cake on each plate, set a steak on top, and spoon the hot sauce around or over the steak. Make a cross of 2 stems of chives on top of each steak.

Pan-Fried Pork Chops with Apple and Sage en Papillote

This is a perfect and easy supper recipe. The pork is cooked in a foil parcel, and it actually makes the sauce while it cooks, which cuts down on the work – and even the washing up.

1 tablespoon sunflower oil
4 large pork chops, well trimmed of fat
2 teaspoons runny honey
salt and freshly ground black pepper
15g (½ oz) butter
1 large onion, thinly sliced

2 dessert apples, peeled, cored and sliced into wedges
100ml (4 fl oz) apple juice
1 x 125ml carton full-fat crème fraîche
8 fresh sage leaves, chopped, plus extra whole leaves, to garnish

Preheat the oven to 190°C/Fan 170°C/Gas 5.

1 Heat a large frying pan until hot, then add the oil. Spread each chop with a half-teaspoon of honey and season well. Brown the chops in the pan for about 1 minute on each side, or until golden, then remove from the pan and set aside.

2 Heat the butter in the pan, add the onion and fry for 2–3 minutes. Add the apple and cook for another 3 minutes, then pour in the apple juice, crème fraîche and chopped sage. Bring up to the boil, season and simmer for 2 minutes.

3 Make 4 x 25cm (10 in) foil squares. Place 1 chop on one half of each foil square. Divide the onion and apple mixture evenly over the chops. Fold over the foil and seal the edges together (like a Cornish pasty).

4 Place on a baking sheet and bake in the preheated oven for 15–18 minutes, or until cooked through and there are no pink juices.

5 Rest for 2–3 minutes before serving. Open up the foil, decorate with sage leaves and serve in the parcel.

Lamb Paysanne with English Root Vegetables

I adore this way of slow-roasting a shoulder of lamb. This is an all-in-one dish: the vegetables and potatoes are cooked at the same time as the lamb. All you need to do is cook a green vegetable separately if you wish.

1.5kg (3 lb 5 oz) whole shoulder of lamb, bone left in
salt and freshly ground black pepper
350g (12 oz) small turnips, peeled and quartered
350g (12 oz) carrots, peeled and thickly sliced
350g (12 oz) potatoes, peeled and cut into 2cm (¾ in) cubes

2 large onions, thickly sliced
2 garlic cloves, roughly chopped
scant 300ml (10 fl oz) white wine
600ml (1 pint) water
leaves from 2 sprigs fresh rosemary, chopped
1 small bunch fresh parsley, chopped

Preheat the oven to 220°C/Fan 200°C/Gas 7.

1 Remove the skin and trim any extra fat from the shoulder. Season well. Lift the lamb into a large roasting tin, skin side down, and brown in the preheated oven for about 30 minutes, turning over halfway so that both sides are brown.

2 Transfer the lamb to a plate, and then add all the remaining ingredients except for the parsley to the hot roasting tin. Return the lamb to the tin, on top of the vegetables, then cover with foil. Reduce the temperature to 150°C/Fan 130°C/Gas 2, and slowly cook for 3–4 hours, or until completely tender, and it is falling apart and away from the bone.

3 To serve, lift the meat carefully off the vegetables and slice into thick pieces. Serve with the vegetables and the thin gravy, sprinkled with parsley.

Serves 4–6

TO PREPARE AHEAD

The lamb can be browned 8 hours before the final cooking. The vegetables can be prepared and kept in water up to 8 hours ahead. Not suitable for freezing.

TO COOK IN THE AGA

Brown the lamb in the roasting tin at the top of the Roasting Oven for about 20 minutes, turning halfway through to brown both sides. At step 2, cover the tin with foil and return to the Roasting Oven for about 15 minutes, then transfer to the Simmering Oven for about 4 hours, or until completely tender and the lamb is falling off the bone.

Serves 6

TO PREPARE AHEAD

The meat can be put in the marinade (step 1) and all the ingredients can be prepared 24 hours ahead. Keep them all in the fridge. Not suitable for freezing.

TO COOK IN THE AGA

Cook on the Boiling Plate. Soften the onion, covered, in the Simmering Oven for about 15 minutes.

Yellow Thai Beef

As this recipe involves such a short cooking time for the beef, you need to use a prime cut such as rump or sirloin, well trimmed. If time allows, you will find it is easier to slice the beef thinly if you freeze it for about 10 minutes first. Yellow Thai paste is sold in little jars and you can usually find it in supermarkets in the ethnic section. Serve with boiled rice.

700g (1½ lb) rump steak, cut into very thin slices
1–2 tablespoons sunflower oil
1 large onion, thinly sliced
1 good tablespoon yellow Thai paste, from a jar
1 x 400ml carton or can coconut milk
1 small red chilli, seeds removed, and thinly sliced
finely grated zest and juice of ½ lime
175g (6 oz) fresh baby corn, sliced on the diagonal

1 level tablespoon cornflour
3 tablespoons cold water
1 x 220g can water chestnuts, drained and each cut into 3
salt and freshly ground black pepper
chopped fresh coriander, to serve

MARINADE
2 tablespoons soy sauce
2 tablespoons dry or medium sherry
1 tablespoon runny honey

1 In a bowl, mix together the marinade ingredients and add the slices of beef. Marinate for a minimum of 20 minutes.
2 Drain the beef, discarding the marinade. Heat a large frying pan over a high heat, add the oil and when very hot add the beef. Stir-fry for 2–3 minutes, or until brown (you may need to do this in batches). Remove the beef with a slotted spoon and set aside.
3 Lower the temperature under the pan, add the onion and cook for about 10 minutes until almost soft. Add the Thai paste and fry for 1 minute. Stir in the coconut milk, chilli, lime zest and baby corn. Simmer for about 4 minutes, stirring occasionally.
4 Slake the cornflour with the cold water and pour into the pan, stirring all the time until it starts to thicken.
5 Stir in the browned beef, water chestnuts and some seasoning. Cook, stirring, for about 3–4 minutes or until thickened. If a little too thick, add a touch more water.
6 When piping hot, stir in the lime juice and check the seasoning. Serve hot, sprinkled with the coriander.

Vegetarian

It never worries me when I hear a potential guest is vegetarian. My daughter Annabel prefers vegetarian food, and it has been fun developing ideas that might please her – and others at the same time! Quite a few of these vegetarian recipes would appeal to meat-eaters as well, because the flavours are so good. I don't think many people would turn down a wild mushroom and garlic tart, or a portion of our lovely butternut squash and spinach risotto.

The recipes here use not just vegetables, but pulses such as lentils, grains such as rice, plus pasta, noodles and pastry, which bulk the vegetables out. Flavour is vital when cooking vegetarian dishes, and these recipes include a huge variety. You may feel that all the cutting, chopping and peeling of veg for vegetarian dishes is a chore, but that, too, you can do in advance – yet another potential stress gone.

The simple omelette traditionally served to vegetarians need not appear ever again with so many ideas to choose from. But, I must admit, I have included an omelette, although it is in the form of a very elegant frittata loaf ...

For more vegetarian ideas, see:

Wild Mushroom and Garlic Tarts

These look so attractive, and are perfect as a main course for lunch or as a starter. If you can get it, use puff pastry made with butter – I have found it the best.

2 medium onions, quartered
salt and freshly ground black
   pepper
25g (1 oz) butter
300g (10 oz) mixed wild
   mushrooms, sliced
2 garlic cloves, crushed

1 x 375g packet ready-rolled puff
   pastry
1 large egg, beaten
50g (2 oz) Gruyère cheese,
   grated
1 tablespoon fresh thyme leaves

Preheat the oven to 200°C/Fan 180°C/Gas 6.

1 Boil the onion quarters in salted water for about 5 minutes and drain. Dry thoroughly on kitchen paper.

2 Melt the butter in a large frying pan and fry the boiled onion, mushrooms and garlic over a high heat for about 5 minutes, or until there is no liquid left in the pan. Season well and set aside to cool.

3 Roll out the pastry on a floured surface and cut out 4 circles about 14cm (5½ in) in diameter. Chill in the fridge while the mushrooms cool.

4 Lay the pastry circles on a baking sheet. Brush a border around the pastry of about 1cm (½ in) with the beaten egg. Spoon the mushroom mixture into the middle of the circles, top with cheese and bake in the preheated oven for about 20 minutes, or until the pastry is golden brown and puffed up.

5 Sprinkle with the thyme and serve hot.

Makes 4 tarts, to serve 4

TO PREPARE AHEAD
Prepare to step 3 up to 24 hours ahead. Not suitable for freezing.

TO COOK IN THE AGA
Bake on the floor of the Roasting Oven for about 15 minutes.

Garlic, Cheese and Roast Vegetable Naan Bread

A wonderful light supper or lunch dish served with green salad. You could also use this topping on pitta bread or on bruschetta.

1 red pepper
1 yellow pepper
1 aubergine, sliced
1 medium onion, sliced
2 tablespoons olive oil
salt and freshly ground black
  pepper

1 x 85g Boursin cheese (with
  garlic and herbs)
4 mini naan breads
a few drops balsamic vinegar
chopped fresh parsley

Preheat the oven to 220°C/Fan 200°C/Gas 7. Grease a large roasting tin or line with non-stick baking paper.

1 Quarter the peppers lengthways, remove the seeds, and cut the flesh into chunky pieces.

2 Mix all the vegetables together in another large roasting tin with the olive oil and season. Roast the vegetables for 20–25 minutes in the preheated oven, turning over halfway through the cooking time, or until charred.

3 Spread a quarter of the garlic and herb cheese over each naan bread. Divide the lightly charred vegetables between the cheese bases. Transfer to the prepared roasting tin.

4 Bake in the preheated oven for approximately 10 minutes, or until hot right through and crisp. Drizzle with the balsamic vinegar, sprinkle with the parsley and serve immediately.

Makes 4

TO PREPARE AHEAD
Prepare to the end of step 3 up to 12 hours in advance. Not suitable for freezing.

TO COOK IN THE AGA
At step 2, roast the vegetables on the floor of the Roasting Oven, turning over halfway, for 20–25 minutes, or until charred. Alternatively, grill them in 2 batches on the hot grill pan of the Boiling Plate. At step 4, cook on the second set of runners in the Roasting Oven for about 10 minutes.

Italian Garden Lasagne

Serves 8–10

TO PREPARE AHEAD

Complete up to the end of step 4, cover and keep in the fridge for up to 2 days. Freeze at the end of step 4 for up to 2 months.

TO COOK IN THE AGA

Make the two sauces on the Boiling Plate. At step 5, bake near to the top of the Roasting Oven for about 25–35 minutes, or until golden brown and piping hot.

This is ideal for a buffet as it is totally vegetarian, yet meat-eaters will love it too. It is important to season the vegetables well. Lasagne sheets vary in size so you may need more or fewer. When layering the sheets of pasta, do not overlap them.

about 8 sheets (225g/8 oz) dried
  lasagne
75g (3 oz) Parmesan, grated

CHEESE SAUCE
1.1 litres (2 pints) full-fat milk
1 bay leaf
2–3 black peppercorns
75g (3 oz) butter
75g (3 oz) flour
salt and freshly ground black
  pepper
1 tablespoon Dijon mustard
175g (6 oz) mature Cheddar,
  grated

TOMATO AND MUSHROOM
SAUCE
3 tablespoons sunflower oil

2 large onions, roughly chopped
2 red peppers, seeded and
  roughly chopped
3 fat garlic cloves, crushed
40g (1½ oz) plain flour
3 x 400g cans chopped tomatoes
900g (2 lb) chestnut mushrooms,
  sliced
4 tablespoons tomato purée
1 bunch fresh basil, roughly
  chopped
1 tablespoon caster sugar
salt and freshly ground black
  pepper

Preheat the oven to 200°C/Fan 180°C/Gas 6. You will need a large shallow ovenproof dish 36 x 25 x 5cm (14 x 10 x 2 in).

1 First infuse the milk for the cheese sauce. Measure the milk into a pan, add the bay leaf and peppercorns, and bring slowly up to just below boiling point. Remove from the heat, cover and allow to infuse while you make the tomato sauce.

2 Make the tomato and mushroom sauce. Heat the oil in a large, deep frying pan, add the onions, pepper and garlic, and fry for 2–3 minutes, or until the onion starts to soften. Stir in the flour, then blend in the

Mary Berry's Stress-free Kitchen

tomatoes. Bring to the boil, stirring, until thickened. Add the mushrooms and the tomato purée, basil and sugar. Bring back to the boil and simmer for 5 minutes. Season well and set aside while making the cheese sauce.

3 Next make the cheese sauce. Strain the infused milk. Melt the butter in a large saucepan. Add the flour, stir well until combined, then gradually blend in the infused milk. Bring up to the boil, stirring all the time until thickened. Season, then add the mustard and Cheddar.

4 Now layer the lasagne so that you have 3 layers of the two sauces and 2 layers of pasta. Start with a layer of the two sauces on the base of the dish. Then add a layer of pasta, more of the sauces, then another layer of pasta. Cover with the tomato sauce, then finally with the cheese sauce. Sprinkle with Parmesan.

5 Cook in the preheated oven for about 35–45 minutes, or until golden brown on top and bubbling and hot in the middle.

Serves 4–6

TO PREPARE AHEAD
Can be made the day before, up to the end of step 5, and kept in the fridge. Not suitable for freezing.

TO COOK IN THE AGA
At step 5, slide the dish on to the top set of runners in the Roasting Oven and bake for about 15–20 minutes, or until bubbling and the cheese has browned.

Parmigiano di Melanzane

A classic Italian dish that is rarely made at home. In Italy the aubergines would be fried but my version is much lighter.

TOMATO SAUCE
1 tablespoon olive oil
1 large onion, chopped
2 fat garlic cloves, crushed
1 x 500g carton passata
a teaspoon of caster sugar
salt and freshly ground black
  pepper

1 tablespoon fresh basil, chopped

2 medium aubergines
100g (4 oz) mozzarella cheese,
  cut into thin slices
40g (1½ oz) Parmesan, grated

Preheat the oven to 200°C/Fan 180°C/Gas 6. You will need a shallow ovenproof dish about 25 x 19cm (10 x 7½ in).

1 First make the sauce. Heat the oil in a frying pan, add the onion, cover and cook over a low heat for about 10 minutes, or until soft.
2 Meanwhile, bring a pan of salted water to the boil. Trim the stalks from the aubergines and slice thinly. Cook in the boiling, salted water for about 5 minutes, or until soft but still holding their shape. Drain and pat dry on kitchen paper.
3 Add the garlic, passata, sugar, seasoning and basil to the onion. Bring to the boil, then remove from the heat.
4 Pour half the tomato sauce into the ovenproof dish. Lay half the aubergines on top, and season well. Place the slices of mozzarella cheese on top of the aubergine. Lay the remaining slices of aubergine on top of the cheese and pour over the remaining tomato sauce.
5 Sprinkle with the Parmesan and bake in the preheated oven for about 20 minutes, or until bubbling and the cheese has browned. Serve hot.

Courgette and Feta Fritters

I first had something similar for lunch in glorious sunshine in the South of France. They are good on their own with grills or steaks, or for supper with poached or fried eggs and bacon, but they're also great for vegetarians. We grow yellow courgettes, but as they are not always available, just use the green ones.

4 tablespoons sunflower oil
1 large onion, finely chopped
500g (1 lb 2 oz) small green or
   yellow courgettes, trimmed and
   coarsely grated
200g (7 oz) feta cheese
4 tablespoons chopped fresh
   mint
3 large eggs, beaten
40g (1½ oz) plain flour
salt and freshly ground black
   pepper

FRESH TOMATO SAUCE
1 tablespoon sunflower oil
½ onion, finely chopped
2 celery sticks, finely chopped
6 large tomatoes, quartered, or
   1 x 400g can chopped tomatoes
1 teaspoon tomato purée

1 First make the tomato sauce. Heat the oil in a saucepan, add the onion and celery, and stir over a high heat for 2–3 minutes. Add the tomatoes and tomato purée, cover and cook over a low heat for about 20 minutes, or until the vegetables are soft. Strain through a sieve and keep hot.

2 Next prepare the fritters. Heat 1 tablespoon of the oil in a large non-stick frying pan. Add the onion, cover with a lid and soften over a low heat for about 15 minutes.

3 Remove the lid, increase the heat and add the courgettes. Fry with the onion for about 2 minutes or until just softened. Drain through a sieve, pat dry with kitchen paper, then tip into a mixing bowl. Leave to cool.

4 Add the remaining ingredients to the bowl, except for the extra oil, and mix together. Season well.

5 Heat the remaining oil in the large frying pan. Drop spoonfuls of the mixture into the pan (about 3 fritters at a time) and brown on both sides for about 3–4 minutes (you will need to do this in batches).

6 Serve the fritters hot with the tomato sauce.

Makes 12 fritters, to serve 6

TO PREPARE AHEAD

The tomato sauce can be made up to 2 days ahead and kept in the fridge. Brown the fritters (steps 2–5) the day before. To reheat, place on a baking sheet lined with non-stick paper and cook in a preheated oven (200°C/Fan 180°C/Gas 6) for about 10 minutes. Not suitable for freezing.

TO COOK IN THE AGA

Cook the fritters in a frying pan on the Simmering Plate for 3–4 minutes on each side, or until golden brown and cooked through. Or lay a piece of non-stick baking paper on the Simmering Plate, place spoonfuls of the mixture on to the paper and pull the lid down. Cook for 3–4 minutes on each side. Make the tomato sauce on the Boiling Plate, cover and transfer to the Simmering Oven for about 25 minutes, or until soft.

Chinese Noodle and Vegetable Stir-Fry

A very quick, easy dish that is good to serve with grilled chops, spare ribs or fish.

100g (4 oz) medium egg noodles
2 tablespoons olive oil
2 red peppers, thinly sliced
8 spring onions, thinly sliced on the diagonal
2cm (¾ in) piece fresh ginger root, peeled and grated
225g (8 oz) pak choi, thinly sliced, keeping the white and green parts separate
salt and freshly ground black pepper
a handful cashew nuts

SAUCE
1 tablespoon Chinese five-spice powder
2 tablespoons dark soy sauce
2 tablespoons runny honey
1 teaspoon white wine vinegar
salt and freshly ground black pepper

1 Cook the noodles according to the packet instructions, drain and refresh in cold water. Set aside.

2 In a small bowl mix together the sauce ingredients until smooth.

3 Heat the oil in a large non-stick frying pan. Add the peppers, spring onions, ginger and white parts of the pak choi, and fry over a high heat, stirring, for about 4–5 minutes, or until the vegetables are nearly cooked but still crisp.

4 Add the noodles and the green leaves of the pak choi to the pan. Continue to cook over a high heat and stir to combine. Pour over the sauce and season well.

5 Sprinkle in the cashew nuts and remove from the heat. Serve at once, with extra soy sauce if liked.

Serves 4

TO PREPARE AHEAD
All the vegetables can be prepared up to 12 hours ahead, covered with clingfilm and kept in the fridge. The recipe is so quick that it can be stir-fried fresh and on the table in 10 minutes. Not suitable for freezing.

TO COOK IN THE AGA
Cook the noodles and the sauce on the Boiling Plate.

Make ahead to the end of step 4 and keep in the fridge for up to 24 hours. Not suitable for freezing.

TO COOK IN THE AGA

For step 1, cook the onions and vegetables first on the Boiling Plate, then transfer, covered, to the Simmering Oven for 30 minutes or until tender. For step 2, cook the potatoes on the Boiling Plate. For step 5, cook the assembled dish on a high shelf in the Roasting Oven for about 20 minutes, or until golden brown and piping hot.

Lentil and Vegetable Cottage Pie

This recipe was very popular with my family when we were testing ideas. It is not only cheap to produce but tastes delicious.

2 large onions, finely chopped
2 garlic cloves, crushed
2 tablespoons olive oil
3 celery sticks, sliced
2 large carrots, sliced
100g (4 oz) dried red lentils, rinsed
1 x 400g can chopped tomatoes
300ml (10 fl oz) vegetable stock
2 teaspoons sun-dried tomato paste
50g (2 oz) sun-dried tomatoes, drained if in oil, and chopped
salt and freshly ground black pepper

TOPPING
1kg (2¼ lb) old potatoes, peeled
about 150ml (5 fl oz) milk
1 bunch spring onions, finely chopped
25g (1 oz) butter
175g (6 oz) mature Cheddar, grated

Preheat the oven to 200°C/Fan 180°C/Gas 6. You will need a buttered ovenproof dish, about 28 x 23 x 5cm (11 x 9 x 2 in).

1 Cook the onions and garlic in the oil over a low heat in a large pan for about 10 minutes, or until soft. Add the celery and carrots, and cook for a further 5 minutes. Stir in the lentils, then add the chopped tomatoes, stock, tomato paste, sun-dried tomatoes and plenty of seasoning. Bring to the boil, cover and simmer for about 20 minutes, or until the vegetables are tender. Check the seasoning.

2 Meanwhile, cook the potatoes in boiling salted water until tender.

3 While the potatoes are cooking, heat the milk and spring onions together in a small pan and simmer gently for about 5 minutes, or until the spring onions are soft. Drain the potatoes well, then add the warm milk with the spring onions, and the butter. Mash together, adding plenty of seasoning. Stir in two-thirds of the grated cheese and check the seasoning.

4 Spoon the vegetable mixture into the prepared dish and gently spread the potato on top. Scatter over the remaining cheese.

5 Cook in the preheated oven for about 30 minutes, or until the potato is golden and the sauce bubbling.

Butternut Squash and Spinach Risotto

Very good on its own or with a fresh green salad. Having cut the squash in half and removed the seeds, I find it easier to cut the flesh into half-rings and then remove the skin. Removing the tough skin as a whole piece is hard work!

900g (2 lb) butternut squash
2 tablespoons olive oil
1 bunch salad onions, finely
 chopped
2 garlic cloves, crushed
225g (8 oz) arborio risotto rice
75ml (2½ fl oz) white wine

about 1 litre (35 fl oz) vegetable
 stock
225g (8 oz) baby spinach,
 roughly chopped
salt and freshly ground black
 pepper
2 tablespoons grated Parmesan

1 Cut the squash in half lengthways and remove the seeds. Slice into half-rings and cut off the skin. Cut the flesh evenly into 1cm (½ in) cubes.

2 Heat the oil in a large non-stick frying pan and gently fry the squash, salad onions and garlic for about 4 minutes, stirring from time to time. Do not allow to colour.

3 Add the rice and stir constantly over a high heat for about 2 minutes. Pour in the wine and bring to a gentle boil, stirring frequently until the liquid has been absorbed by the rice.

4 Measure the stock into a separate pan and heat to simmering point. Gradually add ladlefuls of stock to the rice, and continue to cook after each ladleful for 2–3 minutes, stirring constantly, until the stock is absorbed and the rice is creamy and just tender, about 10–15 minutes.

5 Stir in the spinach, adding a little more hot stock if necessary. The amount of stock required can vary, depending on how fast you cook the risotto and the width of the pan. Season to taste.

6 Cover and leave to stand for 2–3 minutes before serving. Sprinkle with the Parmesan and serve hot.

Serves 4–6

TO PREPARE AHEAD
Have all the ingredients prepared up to 24 hours ahead. Then the risotto will only take about 20 minutes to make. Not suitable for freezing.

TO COOK IN THE AGA
Cook as above on the Simmering Plate.

TO PREPARE AHEAD
The frittata can be made on the morning of serving. It is not suitable for reheating or for freezing.

TO COOK IN THE AGA
Soften the onion, covered, in the Simmering Oven. Continue on the Boiling Plate. Bake on the second set of runners in the Roasting Oven for about 12 minutes.

Frittata Terrine

A frittata is usually made in a frying pan, but for a change this one is made in a loaf tin, as it looks so good. It's also easy to portion into slices, which makes it very useful for picnics.

1 tablespoon olive oil
1 large onion, finely chopped
1 red pepper, seeded and finely chopped
1 small courgette, finely chopped
5 large eggs
25g (1 oz) Parmesan, grated
1 small bunch fresh chives, snipped
salt and freshly ground black pepper

Preheat the oven to 180°C/Fan 160°C/Gas 4. Grease or line a 450g (1 lb) loaf tin with non-stick baking paper.

1 Heat the oil in a frying pan, add the onion, cover and cook over a medium heat for about 5–10 minutes, or until starting to soften.
2 Add the pepper and courgette, and fry for a further 5 minutes.
3 Beat the eggs in a jug, add the Parmesan and chives, and pour into the pan with the vegetables. Stir and season well. Pour into the prepared loaf tin.
4 Slide the tin into the centre of the preheated oven and bake for about 15 minutes, or until the mixture has just set in the middle (be careful not to overcook or it will be rubbery). Leave to cool for about 10 minutes, then tip upside down on to a serving platter. Remove the paper.
5 Serve while warm, in slices, with Tomato Sauce (see page 107) if liked.

Sides

Sides are side dishes or main-course accompaniments, usually consisting of vegetables. Vegetables are not only hugely nutritious but also immensely versatile. You can eat them by themselves, or as a delicious accompaniment to protein main courses. There are some traditional vegetable recipes here, but others are more unusual – I've included some ideas for cooking veg en papillote (this means cooked in a foil wrap, and no last-minute pans to wash up) – and they don't just include vegetables. There is a couscous salad, for instance.

Vegetables are usually thought of as a last-minute job, but in my stress-free kitchen there is lots you can do in advance. You could part-cook roast veg the day before, for instance, then blast them in a hot oven on the day. Salads are thought of as last-minute as well, but the essential elements can be prepared in advance – the washing of the leaves, the making of the dressing. Pour the dressing in the bottom of the bowl, then put in the less-tender leaves, saving the tenderest floppy leaves – like round lettuce, lamb's lettuce and pea shoots – for last. Then all you have to do at the last minute is toss. Veg purées are very useful too to make cooking relaxed and easy; simply blitz the veg in a food processor when tender. Make well in advance, and reheat in the oven covered with foil when baking or roasting the main course.

For more ideas on sides, see:

Oven-Roasted English Roots

A prepare-ahead vegetable dish that needs very little last-minute attention. Vary it with other English root vegetables, such as sweet potatoes, turnips and swede. If you can't get shallots, use small onions, cutting them in half if need be.

350g (12 oz) parsnips, peeled
  (prepared weight)
350g (12 oz) butternut squash,
  peeled and seeded (prepared
  weight)
350g (12 oz) tiny shallots, peeled
  and left whole (prepared
  weight)
350g (12 oz) carrots, peeled
  (prepared weight)

2–3 tablespoons olive oil, plus
  extra for brushing
salt and freshly ground black
  pepper
1 large sprig fresh rosemary,
  leaves only, chopped
chopped fresh parsley

Preheat the oven to 200°C/Fan 180°C/Gas 6. Line a large roasting tin with foil and brush with oil.

1 Cut the parsnips and squash into neat pieces a similar size to the shallots. Slice the carrots on the diagonal (cut them smaller than the other vegetables as they take longer to cook).
2 Bring the vegetables to the boil in salted water to cover, and simmer for 5 minutes. Drain, coat with the oil and season well.
3 Tip the vegetables into the prepared roasting tin and add the rosemary. Roast in the preheated oven for about 40–50 minutes, turning from time to time, until tender, piping hot, golden brown and crisp.
4 Serve sprinkled with the parsley.

TO PREPARE AHEAD

At step 3, par-roast the vegetables the day before for about 30 minutes, but slightly under-brown. Complete the roasting in a preheated oven at the same temperature for about 30 minutes until piping hot, golden brown and crisp. Not suitable for freezing.

TO COOK IN THE AGA

Cook the vegetables in the roasting tin on the floor of the Roasting Oven for about 40 minutes, turning from time to time, until tender and golden.

Roasted Mediterranean Vegetables with Balsamic Dressing

Roasted vegetables are not only perfect to serve hot with a main course, but also make a great salad for a picnic or barbecue – whether hot or cold.

For a delicious salad variation, follow the recipe, but add to the cold roasted vegetables 50g (2 oz) sun-blushed tomatoes, 225g (8 oz) goat's cheese or mozzarella, cut into cubes, and the torn leaves of a large bunch of basil. Toss well and serve chilled.

350g (12 oz) aubergines (two medium), cut into thin slices
350g (12 oz) courgettes, cut into 4 x 1 cm (1½ x ½ in) batons
2 red peppers, seeds removed, and cut into chunks
2 yellow peppers, seeds removed, and cut into chunks
1 large onion, peeled and cut into thick wedges
2 garlic cloves, with skins left on
3 tablespoons oil
salt and freshly ground black pepper
2 tablespoons balsamic vinegar

Preheat the oven to 220°C/Fan 200°C/Gas 7.

1 In a large bowl, toss the prepared vegetables and garlic in the oil. Season well.

2 Tip into a large roasting tin and roast in the preheated oven for about 30 minutes, or until golden brown and just tender. Stir once halfway through cooking.

3 Remove the roasted garlic cloves, peel and turn into a bowl, mashing with the back of a teaspoon into a paste. Add the balsamic vinegar to the garlic and mix together. Pour over the hot vegetables and serve at once.

Roasted Spiced Aubergine Salad

Delicious served cold with barbecued or cold meats. This is especially popular with the young and non meat-eaters.

4 large aubergines, cut into 4cm (1½ in) cubes
4 tablespoons olive oil
salt and freshly ground black pepper
1 large onion, chopped
1 teaspoon mixed spice
1 teaspoon medium curry powder

1 teaspoon garam masala
1 x 400g can chopped tomatoes
juice of ½ lemon
1 small bunch fresh coriander, chopped
1 small bunch fresh mint, chopped

Preheat the oven to 200°C/Fan 180°C/Gas 6.

1 Tip the prepared aubergine and 3 tablespoons of the oil into a large roasting tin and mix together, seasoning well. Roast in the preheated oven for about 30 minutes, or until golden brown and soft, turning from time to time.

2 Heat the remaining oil in a large non-stick frying pan, add the onion, cover and gently soften for about 10 minutes. Remove the lid and cook to drive off any liquid in the pan.

3 Add the spices to the onion and fry for 2–3 minutes. Add the tomatoes and soft aubergine. Simmer for about 10 minutes. uncovered, then season well and set aside to become cold.

4 Chill until needed. Just before serving, stir in the lemon juice and fresh herbs.

Serves 6

TO PREPARE AHEAD
Can be made to the end of step 3 up to 12 hours ahead and kept in the fridge. Not suitable for freezing.

TO COOK IN THE AGA
Roast the aubergines on the floor of the Roasting Oven for about 25 minutes. Soften the onion, covered, in the Simmering Oven for about 15 minutes. Continue on the Boiling Plate.

TO PREPARE AHEAD

Cut the potatoes into squares as at the end of step 3, put on well-buttered paper on a baking sheet, cover with clingfilm and keep in the fridge for up to 24 hours. Can be frozen only if made with cream, not stock, for up to 1 month.

TO COOK IN THE AGA

At step 3, bake on the lowest set of runners in the Roasting Oven, covered with buttered paper, for about 45 minutes. Turn around halfway through the cooking time. At step 4, reheat on the second set of runners in the Roasting Oven for 10 minutes.

Dauphinoise Potato Squares

A wonderful way to serve up potatoes that can be prepared ahead and reheated to serve. Traditionally, dauphinoise potatoes are made with cream, which is delicious but rather rich. If this is how you like them, replace the stock with 450ml (15 fl oz) double cream. The advantage here is that although they do not freeze successfully if made with stock, they do freeze well if made with cream.

a little melted butter, for brushing
1.4kg (3 lb) old potatoes, washed
1 garlic clove, crushed
450ml (15 fl oz) chicken stock, or water plus 2 chicken stock cubes
salt and freshly ground black pepper
a little chopped fresh parsley

Preheat the oven to 200°C/Fan 180°C/Gas 6. You will need a small roasting tin, about 30 x 23cm (12 x 9 in).

1 Line the base and sides of the tin with greaseproof or non-stick baking paper and brush generously with melted butter.
2 Peel and thinly slice the potatoes. Blend the crushed garlic with the stock. Arrange the potatoes in the roasting tin in layers. With each layer, add seasoning and pour on some of the stock. Finally, pour some stock over the top.
3 Bake in the preheated oven for about 45–55 minutes, or until tender. Remove from the oven and leave to become completely cold. (The potato is then easier to cut, especially if straight from the fridge.) Once cold, cut into 12 even-sized squares.

Preheat the oven to 200°C/Fan 180°C/Gas 6. Line a baking sheet with non–stick baking paper.

4 Arrange the potato squares on the prepared baking sheet, brush each square with butter and reheat for 15 minutes in the preheated oven, or until piping hot and brown. Scatter with the chopped parsley.

TO PREPARE AHEAD
Can be made up to 24 hours
ahead and kept in the fridge.
Not suitable for freezing.

TO COOK IN THE AGA
Roast the vegetables on the
floor of the Roasting Oven for
about 30 minutes.

Couscous with Roasted Veg and Pesto

There is a good ratio of roasted veg to couscous, which makes this dish look very attractive. The fresh pesto gives it a really distinct flavour. If you have any pesto left, freeze it; some of the colour will be lost but it keeps its flavour.

1 aubergine, diced
1 red pepper, seeded and sliced
1 red onion, thickly sliced
2 small courgettes, thinly sliced
2 garlic cloves, crushed
2 tablespoons olive oil
salt and freshly ground black
  pepper

100g (4 oz) couscous
100ml (4 fl oz) hot vegetable
  stock
4 tablespoons fresh pesto, bought
  or home-made

Preheat the oven to 200°C/Fan 180°C/Gas 6.

1 In a bowl, mix the vegetables and garlic with the oil, season, mix with your hands so all the vegetables are coated in oil then tip into a large roasting tin.

2 Roast in the preheated oven for about 20–30 minutes, or until golden and tender.

3 Measure the couscous into a bowl or jug and pour over the hot stock. Cover with clingfilm and leave to stand for about 5 minutes, or until all the liquid has been absorbed and the couscous has puffed up.

4 Add the roasted vegetables to the couscous and stir in the pesto. Check the seasoning and stir well.

5 Serve either hot or cold. To serve hot, turn into a frying pan and fry with a little oil until piping hot.

Grated Neeps Gratin

Swede, a top favourite in Scotland, is a bit like Marmite: you either love it or you hate it! If you are the former, this will be right up your street.

600g (1 lb 5 oz) swede
50g (2 oz) butter, plus extra for
  greasing
salt and freshly ground black
  pepper

50g (2 oz) fresh white
  breadcrumbs

Preheat the oven to 200°C/Fan 180°C/Gas 6. Butter a shallow ovenproof dish.

1 Using a small knife, remove the thick skin from the swede and discard. Grate the flesh coarsely.

2 Melt the butter in a non-stick frying pan, add the grated swede and season well. Fry for about 5–7 minutes, stirring often.

3 Spoon the swede into the prepared dish, pressing it down evenly.

4 Just before cooking, sprinkle generously with breadcrumbs and bake in the preheated oven for about 30 minutes, or until golden brown and piping hot.

TO PREPARE AHEAD

Make to the end of step 3, and keep in the fridge for up to 24 hours. Not suitable for freezing.

TO COOK IN THE AGA

For step 4, bake on the top set of runners in the Roasting Oven for about 20–25 minutes, or until golden brown.

TO PREPARE AHEAD
Complete to the end of step 2 and keep in the fridge for up to 24 hours. Not suitable for freezing.

TO COOK IN THE AGA
Slide the baking sheet into the Roasting Oven and cook for about 10–12 minutes, or until piping hot.

Sweetheart Cabbage en Papillote

This is such an easy way to cook a vegetable ahead and reheat it. Choose a firm cabbage with bright green outside leaves. One of the major stress-free elements of this recipe is that there is hardly any washing up!

1 large sweetheart (pointed green) cabbage
salt and freshly ground black pepper
25g (1 oz) butter

Preheat the oven to 200°C/Fan 180°C/Gas 6.

1 Slice the cabbage in half and remove the core. Peel off the darker outer leaves, then, using a small knife, cut out and discard the thick vein in the centre of the leaf. Shred these leaves finely. Shred the inner leaves and put in a separate pile.

2 Bring a saucepan of salted water to the boil. Add the dark shredded leaves and boil for 1 minute. Add the white shredded leaves to the water with the outer leaves and boil for 2 minutes. Drain and refresh in cold water until stone cold, then drain really well.

3 Take a piece of foil about 50 x 30cm (19½ x 12 in) and spoon the cabbage on to one side of it. Season well. Sit the butter on top of the cabbage. Fold the foil over the top of the cabbage and seal the edge (like a Cornish pasty).

4 Place on a baking sheet and bake in the preheated oven for about 12–15 minutes, or until piping hot. Make a slit in the top of the foil and turn into a heated serving dish.

Cauliflower with Mustard en Papillote

This is an exciting way to serve cauliflower, and one of its great advantages is that it can be prepared ahead, exactly like the sweetheart cabbage opposite; like the cabbage, it is not suitable for freezing. The method for cooking in the Aga is also the same as for the cabbage.

1 large cauliflower
salt and freshly ground black
  pepper

3 tablespoons full fat crème
  fraîche
1 tablespoon grainy mustard

Preheat the oven to 200°C/Fan 180°C/Gas 6.

1 Break off the small florets from the cauliflower stalk.
2 Bring a saucepan of salted water to the boil. Add the florets and boil for 3–4 minutes, or until just tender. Drain and refresh in cold water until stone cold, then drain again really well.
3 Return the florets to the saucepan, and add the crème fraîche, mustard and seasoning. Without reheating, stir until coated.
4 Wrap in foil, and bake and serve as for the cabbage recipe.

Serves 4–6

TO PREPARE AHEAD
Complete to the end of step 2 and keep in the fridge for up to 24 hours. Not suitable for freezing.

TO COOK IN THE AGA
Slide the baking sheet into the Roasting Oven and cook for about 10–12 minutes, or until piping hot.

Salad of Green Leaves with Broad Beans and Mint Dressing

This stunning-looking salad can be served on a warm day as a meal in its own right, with crusty bread. Alternatively, it makes a lovely change from a classic green salad. If you can't get red chicory, use ordinary green chicory.

225g (8 oz) fresh podded or
  frozen broad beans
2 Little Gem lettuces
2 heads red chicory
50g (2 oz) rocket
100g (4 oz) feta cheese
50g (2 oz) pumpkin seeds

FRESH MINT DRESSING
3 tablespoons white wine vinegar
6 tablespoons olive oil
1 good tablespoon caster sugar
2 tablespoons chopped fresh
  mint

1 Cook the broad beans in boiling salted water for 5 minutes, drain, and refresh in cold water. Then peel away and discard the shells so that you are left with the inner green beans.

2 Wash the lettuces and chicory, and break the leaves into large pieces. Turn into a large salad bowl or serving platter. Add the rocket and mix together. Sprinkle over the cold broad beans. Crumble over the feta and add the pumpkin seeds.

3 In a small jug, mix together the dressing ingredients. Just before serving, pour it over the leaves. Toss together and serve at once.

Serves 4–6

TO PREPARE AHEAD

The beans can be cooked and shelled ahead. The leaves, feta and pumpkin seeds can all be arranged in a bowl, covered in clingfilm and kept in the fridge for up to 6 hours ahead. The dressing can be made and kept in a jar up to 12 hours ahead. Toss the salad with the dressing just before serving. Not suitable for freezing.

TO COOK IN THE AGA

Cook the broad beans on the Boiling Plate.

Puddings and Desserts

Hot or cold, satisfying or elegant, there is a huge choice here – tarts, mousses, salads, ice creams, pavlovas and meringues, as well as a trifle. Most of the puds here can be prepared ahead: with one course virtually ready, needing little other than reheating or finishing off at the last moment, you will be less stressed about the rest of your menu. You can relax and concentrate better!

Hot puddings might be thought of as fattening, but you wouldn't be eating them every day – and a treat to look forward to is one way of relieving stress! Cold desserts, based on fruit, are less calorific perhaps, but still as much of a treat – and some cold sweets, particularly the summer pud and the ice cream, need to be prepared in advance. I've written about this before, but when serving ice creams you can scoop them out into balls in advance and put back in the freezer. This saves time and stress at the last minute.

TO PREPARE AHEAD
**Complete to the end of step 4.
Freeze for up to 1 month. Ten
minutes before serving, take
out as many as you need to
decorate.**

Iced Lemon Flummery

*This without doubt is the most asked-for pud from our Aga
workshop days. It's fast to make – no cooking at all – and very
refreshing to eat, and is served still frozen like a sorbet. As in many
of my desserts, it is served in individual dishes, which I think makes
serving desserts so much simpler.*

FLUMMERY
300ml (10 fl oz) double cream
finely grated zest and juice
  of 2 lemons
350g (12 oz) caster sugar
600ml (1 pint) full-fat milk

TOPPING
150ml (5 fl oz) whipping cream,
  whipped
8–12 sprigs fresh mint or
  lemon balm

**You will need a shallow 1.5 litre (2½ pint) plastic container with
a lid.**

1 Pour the double cream into a bowl and whisk until it forms soft
peaks. Stir in the lemon zest, juice, sugar and milk, and mix well until
thoroughly blended.
2 Pour into the container, and cover with a lid. Freeze for at least 6
hours, or until very firm.
3 Working quickly, cut the frozen cream into chunks and process in a
processor until smooth and creamy.
4 Pour into individual ramekin dishes, stand the ramekins on a large flat
platter or sheet, cover with clingfilm and return to the freezer overnight.
5 To serve, spoon a small blob of cream on top of each ramekin and
decorate with a sprig of mint or lemon balm.

Rosy-Pink Fresh Fruit Salad

Serves 6

A lovely pink fruit salad. There's no sugar syrup to make, just a simple raspberry coulis sauce. Vary the fruit depending on the season. This also works beautifully with a strawberry coulis.

PREPARE AHEAD
The complete fruit salad can be kept chilled in the fridge for up to 12 hours. Not suitable for freezing.

1 small ripe melon (cantaloupe
  or charentais)
2 ripe mangoes
1 papaya
2 ripe nectarines or peaches

RASPBERRY COULIS
250g (9 oz) fresh raspberries
icing sugar, to taste

1 Set aside about 1 cupful of raspberries for the fruit salad.

2 Whizz the remaining raspberries in a processor, then pass through a sieve to make a smooth purée. Discard the pips. Add icing sugar to taste. If you do not have a processor, mash the raspberries in a bowl and then pass through a sieve and continue.

3 Peel and seed the melon, and cut the flesh into neat cubes. Peel and stone the mangoes, and peel and seed the papaya. Cut the flesh of both nectarines or peaches into pieces the same size as the melon. It is probably not necessary to peel them unless the skin is really tough; just remove the stones and slice the flesh into wedges.

4 Tip all the fruits together into a serving bowl and mix. Add the raspberry coulis and fold in until all the fruit is coated.

5 Chill for at least 2 hours. Just before serving, add the reserved raspberries.

Raspberry and Almond Trifle

*If you haven't got any sherry or Framboise, use Kirsch or vodka.
Supermarkets now sell really good vanilla custard in cartons in
varying quantities, but be sure to buy the best you can. If you
cannot buy toasted almonds, toast them yourself in a dry pan over
a medium heat on the hob or on a baking sheet under a hot grill.
They will release their natural oil and become brown, but don't
take your eyes off them for a second as they can quickly burn.*

*350g (12 oz) fresh or frozen
  raspberries*
*100ml (4 fl oz) medium dry
  sherry or Framboise (raspberry
  liqueur)*
*1 packet trifle sponges,
  containing 8 sponges*
raspberry jam

*about 10 ratafia biscuits or
  macaroons, coarsely crushed*
*600ml (1 pint) bought vanilla
  custard*
*150ml (5 fl oz) double cream,
  whipped*
*a handful of flaked almonds,
  toasted*

**You will need a shallow dish, preferably glass, about 20cm (8 in)
in diameter, and 6cm (2½ in) deep.**

1 Put the raspberries in a bowl, pour over the sherry or Framboise,
leave for about 10 minutes or, if using frozen raspberries, until thawed.
2 Split the sponges in half and sandwich together with raspberry jam.
Arrange in the base of the dish.
3 Spoon over the raspberries, sprinkle over the crushed ratafia biscuits,
and level gently with the back of a metal spoon.
4 Carefully pour over the custard.
5 Decorate with blobs of softly whipped cream and sprinkle with the
flaked almonds. Serve chilled.

Lime Meringue Roulade

A meringue roulade is quicker and easier to make than a lemon meringue pie, and is just as popular. It also freezes extremely well, stuffed and rolled, which makes it perfect for entertaining.

5 large egg whites
300g (10 oz) caster sugar
50g (2 oz) flaked almonds

grated zest and juice of 1 small lime
2 generous tablespoons lime or lemon curd

FILLING
300ml (10 fl oz) double cream

Preheat the oven to 190°C/Fan 170°C/Gas 5. You will need a Swiss roll tin 30 x 23cm (12 x 9 in), lined with greased, non-stick baking paper.

1 First make the meringue. Whisk the egg whites in an electric mixer on full speed until very stiff. Gradually add the sugar, 1 teaspoon at a time, still on high speed, whisking well between each addition. Whisk until very, very stiff and shiny, and all the sugar has been added.

2 Spread the meringue mixture into the prepared tin and sprinkle with the almonds. Bake in the centre of the preheated oven for about 8–10 minutes, or until pale golden. Reduce the heat to 160°C/Fan 140°C/Gas 3 and cook for a further 15 minutes, or until firm to the touch.

3 Remove from the oven and turn out, almond side down, on to a sheet of non-stick baking paper. Remove the paper from the base of the cooked meringue and allow to cool for about 10 minutes.

4 While it is cooling, make the filling. Lightly whip the cream, add the lime zest and juice, and fold in the lime or lemon curd. Spread evenly over the meringue. With a knife, make an indentation 1cm (½ in) in on one of the long sides, then roll up the meringue fairly tightly from the long end to form a roulade, using the paper to help you roll. If you want a fatter meringue, roll up from one of the short ends. It is essential to roll tightly and firmly at the beginning. Expect the roulade to crack, which is part of its charm.

5 Wrap in non-stick baking paper and chill for about 2 hours before serving – with raspberries if liked.

TO PREPARE AHEAD

Complete to the end of step 4 the day before, and keep in the fridge. Freeze at the end of step 4 for up to 2 months.

TO COOK IN THE AGA

2-oven Aga: At step 2, put the tin on the grid shelf on the floor of the Roasting Oven with the cold plain shelf on the second set of runners and bake for about 8 minutes, or until pale golden. Then transfer to the Simmering Oven, and bake the roulade for a further 15 minutes, or until slightly crisp and firm to the touch. The roulade does expand, so take care of the edges when transferring.

3- or 4-oven Aga: At step 2, put the tin on the grid shelf on the floor of the Baking Oven with the cold plain shelf on the second set of runners and bake for about 8 minutes, or until pale golden. Then transfer to the Simmering Oven, and bake the roulade for a further 15 minutes, or until slightly crisp and firm to the touch.

TO PREPARE AHEAD

Prepare to the end of step 2. Cover and keep in the fridge for up to 24 hours. To freeze, prepare to the end of step 2 and freeze in the ramekins for up to 6 weeks.

TO COOK IN THE AGA

2-oven Aga: Bake on the grid shelf on the floor of the Roasting Oven with the cold plain shelf on the second set of runners for 15 minutes, or until the top of the pudding is set firm and shrinking away from the sides of the dish.

3- or 4-oven Aga: Bake on the grid shelf on the floor of the Baking Oven for about 12–15 minutes, or until the top of the pudding is set firm and shrinking away from the sides of the dish.

Double Chocolate Puddings

This is a wonderful dessert, which can be prepared ahead but is best cooked to serve straightaway. The outside of the dessert is sponge-like and inside is a lovely runny middle. You have the choice of either serving the puddings in the ramekins or turning them out.

50g (2 oz) cocoa powder, sifted
6 tablespoons boiling water
100ml (4 fl oz) milk
3 large eggs
175g (6 oz) self-raising flour
1 rounded teaspoon baking
 powder
100g (4 oz) softened butter, plus
 extra for greasing
300g (10 oz) caster sugar
200g (7 oz) plain chocolate,
 broken into squares
icing sugar, for dusting
single cream, to serve

Preheat the oven to 200°C/Fan 180°C/Gas 6. You will need 10 x size 1 (9cm/3½ in, 5 fl oz) ramekins.

1 Butter and line the bases of the ramekins with buttered non-stick baking paper. There is no need to line the bases if you do not intend to turn out the puddings.

2 Put the cocoa in the processor or mixer, switch on the motor and carefully spoon in the boiling water. Blend for 1–2 minutes, then scrape down the sides of the bowl and add the milk, eggs, flour, baking powder, butter and sugar. Process again until the mixture has become a smooth, thickish batter. If you do not have a processor, mix in a bowl using an electric hand whisk. Divide the mixture between the prepared ramekins, and stack 4 squares of chocolate in the centre of each so the squares of chocolate are on top of each other making a tower.

3 Bake in the preheated oven for 12–15 minutes, or until the top of the pudding is set firm and shrinking away from the sides of the ramekins.

4 Serve straight from the oven, dusted with the icing sugar, or allow to settle for 4–5 minutes, turn out and dust with icing sugar. Serve hot with a little single cream.

Pear Frangipane Tart

This is a great tart to serve for a party. I always like to serve pastry tarts warm. Use a bought 500g pack of shortcrust pastry if time is short.

PASTRY
100g (4 oz) butter, cubed
225g (8 oz) plain flour
25g (1 oz) icing sugar, sifted
1 egg, beaten

FILLING
175g (6 oz) soft butter
175g (6 oz) caster sugar
3 large eggs, beaten
175g (6 oz) ground almonds

40g (1½ oz) plain flour
1 teaspoon almond extract
2 x 400g cans tinned pears,
  drained well on kitchen paper
apricot jam, melted and sieved,
  for glaze
25g (1 oz) flaked almonds,
  toasted
double cream or crème fraîche,
  to serve

Preheat the oven to 200°C/Fan 180°C/Gas 6. Preheat a baking sheet to get very hot. You will need a flan tin 28cm (11 in) in diameter and about 2.5cm (1 in) deep.

1 If making the pastry by hand, rub the butter into the flour and icing sugar until the mixture resembles breadcrumbs, then stir in the beaten egg and bring together to form a dough. If making in a processor, combine the butter, flour and icing sugar in the bowl, then process until the mixture resembles ground almonds. Pour in the beaten egg and pulse the blade until the dough starts to form a ball around the central stem. Form the pastry into a smooth flat cake, wrap in clingfilm and chill for 30 minutes or until manageable.

2 Make the filling in the unwashed processor. Cream the butter and sugar together, then gradually add the beaten eggs (do not worry if it looks curdled at this stage). Scrape down the sides of the bowl with a spatula. Add the ground almonds, flour and almond extract. Process for 2–3 seconds until well incorporated. If you do not have a processor, beat by hand in a bowl. Leave in the fridge until required.

3 Roll out the chilled pastry on a lightly floured work surface and use to line the flan tin. If time allows, chill for a further 30 minutes.

Serves 10–12

TO PREPARE AHEAD

The cooked pastry-lined flan tin can be kept, covered with clingfilm, in the fridge for up to 24 hours. Filled with the frangipane mixture, it can be kept for about 1 hour, covered and refrigerated. To freeze, complete the tart to the end of step 5 and freeze for up to 1 month.

TO COOK IN THE AGA

2-oven Aga: No need to bake blind in the Aga. At step 5, place the tin on a baking sheet and bake on the floor of the Roasting Oven for 15–20 minutes until pale golden. Then put the cold plain shelf on the second set of runners and continue to bake for a further 15–20 minutes, or until the almond filling is set and golden brown. If the pastry is becoming too dark, place a ring of foil around the edge.

3- or 4-oven Aga: No need to bake blind in the Aga. At step 5, place the tin on a baking sheet and bake on the floor of the Roasting Oven until pale golden, about 15–20 minutes. Then transfer to the centre of the Baking Oven until set and golden brown, for another 15–20 minutes.

4 To bake blind, line the pastry with foil and baking beans. Sit the flan tin on the preheated baking sheet and bake blind in the preheated oven for about 15 minutes. Remove the foil and beans, and bake for a further 5–8 minutes, or until the pastry is pale golden and dry.

5 Spoon the frangipane mixture into the pastry case and level the top using a small palette knife. Arrange the pear halves, cut side down, attractively on the filling. Be sure to leave enough room between them to allow the frangipane to rise. Bake in the preheated oven for about 20 minutes, or until set.

6 Cool slightly, brush with the hot apricot glaze and sprinkle with the toasted flaked almonds. Serve warm with cream or crème fraîche.

Divine Lemon Pots

Probably the easiest dessert you will ever make – and so delicious too! It came my way from a dear friend, Di. Four of us play tennis every Monday and so often swap recipes and ideas over coffee. It has become a firm favourite ever since.

600ml (1 pint) pouring double
  cream
150g (5 oz) caster sugar
finely grated zest and juice of
  3 lemons

16 fresh raspberries
8 leaves fresh mint

You will need 8 small coffee cups, wine glasses, small ramekins or shot glasses.

1 Heat the cream, sugar and lemon zest in a wide-based pan over a low heat until at simmering point. Stir continuously for about 3 minutes until the sugar has dissolved.
2 Remove from the heat and allow to cool slightly (until lukewarm).
3 Mix the lemon juice with the cooled cream in the pan and stir.
4 Pour the lemon cream into the pots and transfer to the fridge to set for a minimum of 2 hours.
5 When set, arrange 2 raspberries on top of each pot and garnish with a mint leaf.

TO PREPARE AHEAD
Complete to the end of step 4 up to 24 hours before serving, and keep in the fridge. Not suitable for freezing.

TO COOK IN THE AGA
Heat the milk on the Simmering Plate of the Aga.

TO PREPARE AHEAD
The soufflés can be made
ahead up to the end of step
5 and kept in the fridge for
6 hours. Cook straight from
the fridge, but being cold
they will take about 5 minutes
longer in the oven. Not
suitable for freezing.

TO COOK IN THE AGA
Bake on the grid shelf on the
floor of the Roasting Oven
for about 8 minutes, or until
risen.

Hot Passion Soufflés

*Very impressive and not nearly as difficult as you may think. Don't
overcook them – they need to be soft in the centre.*

*A point to remember: when a recipe calls for orange juice and it
is cooked – for example, in a soufflé or a sauce – use a good orange
juice from a carton, the sort you have for breakfast. If the recipe
requires no heating and therefore you would get the full fresh
flavour, use freshly squeezed oranges.*

soft butter, for greasing	*1 rounded tablespoon cornflour*
8 passion fruit	*3 large eggs, separated*
about 150 ml (5 fl oz) orange	*100g (4 oz) caster sugar*
juice, from a carton	*icing sugar, for dusting*

***Preheat the oven to 200°C/Fan 180°C/Gas 6. You will need 6 x
size 1 (9cm/3½ in, 5 fl oz) ramekins, and a roasting tin large
enough to hold them without touching.***

1 Generously butter the insides of the ramekins. Cut the passion fruit in
half and scoop out the pulp into a measuring jug. Make up to 225ml
(8 fl oz) with orange juice.

2 In a medium bowl, slake the cornflour with 2 tablespoons of the
orange juice. Heat the remaining juice until boiling. Pour on to the
cornflour mixture, stirring continually, then return to the pan. Bring to
the boil to thicken. Remove from the heat.

3 Whisk the egg whites on full speed with an electric whisk until like a
cloud or soft peaks. Gradually add the sugar, 1 teaspoon at a time, still
whisking on maximum speed, to become stiff and glossy.

4 Beat the egg yolks into the thickened fruit juice. Mix in 2 generous
tablespoons of the meringue to loosen, then finally carefully fold in the
remaining meringue.

5 Divide the mixture between the prepared ramekins and fill to the top.
Level the surface and run the point of a teaspoon around the edge,
pushing the mixture slightly inwards (this will allow it to rise evenly).

6 Gently transfer the ramekins to a small roasting tin. Pour boiling water
halfway up the sides of the ramekins. Carefully transfer to the centre of
the preheated oven and bake for about 10–15 minutes, or until risen.
Dust with icing sugar and serve at once. The centre should still be
slightly soft.

White Chocolate Mousses

Really fast to make and memorable to eat. If you haven't any metal rings, use small empty chopped tomato or baked bean cans. Take off the top and base with a can opener and wash thoroughly.

BASE
50g (2 oz) plain chocolate
75g (3 oz) Hobnob biscuits
  (without chocolate coating),
  coarsely crushed
225g (8 oz) strawberries, thinly
  sliced
8 sprigs fresh mint

WHITE CHOCOLATE MOUSSE
1 x 200g bar 100% Belgian or
  Continental white chocolate,
  broken into small pieces
1 x 200ml carton double cream
1 x 200ml carton full-fat crème
  fraîche

You will need 8 x 7cm (2¾ in) metal rings. Place on a baking sheet lined with non-stick baking paper or clingfilm.

1 Break the plain chocolate into a medium-sized bowl and melt over a pan of hot water. Make sure the bowl does not touch the water and do not allow the chocolate to become too hot. Add the biscuits to the warm melted chocolate, stir to mix, then using the back of a metal spoon press into the bottom of the metal rings. Allow to set in the fridge while making the mousse.

2 For the mousse, put the white chocolate and cream in a bowl and melt over a pan of gently simmering water, stirring until smooth. (Again, make sure the bowl does not touch the water, and do not allow the chocolate to get hot or it will become grainy and will not set.) Stir the crème fraîche into the melted white chocolate and cream, and carefully mix until smooth.

3 Neatly arrange the strawberry slices up the sides of the rings and spoon the mousse mixture on to the individual biscuit bases. Gently level the tops. Chill until firm for a minimum of 4 hours.

4 Transfer to a plate, remove from the rings and decorate with the mint.

TO PREPARE AHEAD
Complete to the end of step 3, up to 12 hours ahead, cover and keep in their rings in the fridge. Not suitable for freezing.

TO COOK IN THE AGA
Melt the chocolate in separate bowls on a tea-towel at the back of the Aga several hours ahead.

Serves 6

TO PREPARE AHEAD

At the end of step 4, cover and keep in the fridge for up to 8 hours. To freeze, at the end of step 5, cool the cooked, uniced strudel, then wrap and freeze for up to 3 months.

TO COOK IN THE AGA

At step 5 carefully lift the strudel on to the prepared baking sheet. Slide on to the floor of the Roasting Oven and bake for about 8 minutes, or until the bottom of the pastry is brown. Transfer to the grid shelf on the floor of the Roasting Oven and bake for a further 10–12 minutes, or until golden brown. If getting too brown, slide the cold sheet on to the second set of runners.

Apple, Lemon and Cinnamon Strudel

An apple strudel used to be such a popular recipe, and I think it's worth a comeback. It is so quick and easy to make too. The breadcrumbs help to absorb some of the liquid from the apples and stop the pastry going soggy.

about 6 sheets filo pastry (if the pastry is very thin, use 9 sheets)
about 50g (2 oz) butter, melted
about 25g (1 oz) fresh breadcrumbs

FILLING
1 large cooking apple (about 400g/14 oz peeled weight), peeled, cored and sliced

finely grated zest and juice of ½ lemon
50g (2 oz) demerara sugar
1 teaspoon mixed spice
1 teaspoon ground cinnamon
50g (2 oz) sultanas

ICING
a little lemon juice
175g (6 oz) icing sugar, sieved

Preheat the oven to 190°C/Fan 170°C/Gas 5. Lightly grease a baking sheet.

1 Mix together all the filling ingredients in a bowl.
2 Place 3 sheets of filo, the long sides together, side by side on a board, slightly overlapping in the middle where they join. They should measure altogether about 45 x 31cm (18 x 12 in). Brush with melted butter. Repeat with another 1 or 2 layers, buttering in between them, using the total of 6 or 9 sheets. Sprinkle the top sheets with the breadcrumbs.
3 Spoon the filling into a third of the rectangle at the bottom of one end of the pastry (across the join) about 5cm (2 in) away from the edge and side. Cut away about 2.5cm (1 in) of pastry at the sides, from the top of the filling upwards (this helps prevent too much pastry being folded together).
4 Turn the sides in over the filling and roll up from the filling end into a sausage shape. Carefully lift the strudel on to the prepared baking sheet and brush all over with melted butter.

Mary Berry's Stress-free Kitchen

5 Bake in the preheated oven for about 35–40 minutes, or until the pastry is golden and crisp.

6 Add just enough lemon juice to the sieved icing sugar to blend together (do not make it too runny or it will slide off the strudel). Spread or drizzle in a zigzag pattern over the top of the strudel. Serve immediately with a good vanilla ice cream or crème fraîche.

Quite the Best Summer Pudding

This summer pudding is all fruit and very little bread. I make it fairly shallow in a straight-sided soufflé dish or glass dish. The shallowness means that even though there is much more fruit than bread, the pudding doesn't collapse when turned out. There will be fruit left over, so serve it with the pudding, which should be really well chilled. It needs to be made the day before serving.

350g (12 oz) blackberries
350g (12 oz) blackcurrants
350g (12 oz) redcurrants
1 small punnet, about 150g
 (5 oz) blueberries

350g (12 oz) caster sugar
225g (8 oz) raspberries
8 slices thin-sliced white bread,
 crusts removed
pouring cream, to serve

You will need a 1.1 litre (2 pint) soufflé dish or straight-sided dish, 15 x 8cm (6 x 3 in).

1 Measure all the fruits except the raspberries into a pan with 1 tablespoon water. Add the sugar and bring to the boil, then gently simmer until the fruits are just tender. Cool a little, then add the raspberries.

2 Cut the bread to shapes to fit the base and sides of the dish to about 5cm (2 in) up the side. Dip the bread into the juice first, then line the dish, putting the fruit-soaked side nearest the dish. When the dish is just under half full with fruit, cover with a layer of bread. Add more fruit on top and finally the last slices of bread, spooning a little of the juice over the bread at the top. You should have about 200ml (7 fl oz) of fruit left over to serve with the pudding. Put a small plate on top, press down lightly, then cover with clingfilm and refrigerate overnight.

3 Turn out into a shallow dish a little larger than the summer pudding so that the juices are caught. Serve with the extra reserved fruit and pouring cream.

TO PREPARE AHEAD

Make up to 2 days ahead and keep in the fridge. Serve well chilled, straight from the fridge. Freeze at the end of step 2 for up to 2 months.

TO COOK IN THE AGA

Bring the fruits to the boil on the Boiling Plate, cover and transfer to the Simmering Oven for about 15 minutes, or until the fruits are just tender.

Caramelised Peaches with Brandy

The peaches can also be left whole for this easy recipe, when they look particularly tempting and delicious.

6 fresh peaches or nectarines
soft butter
a little demerara sugar

a little ground cinnamon
6 tablespoons brandy
crème fraîche, to serve

Preheat the oven to 200°C/Fan 180°C/Gas 6.

1 Peel the peaches by dipping into boiling water until the skin is easy to remove (as you would skin a tomato). Nectarines do not need peeling. Cut in half and remove the stones. Dry with kitchen paper, then rub the rounded side of each peach or nectarine with the soft butter.
2 Pack the peaches or nectarines, cut side down, into a dish in which they fit tightly. Sprinkle with demerara sugar and cinnamon, and pour the brandy into the dish around them.
3 Bake in the preheated oven for about 30 minutes, or until tender.
4 Serve hot with crème fraîche.

Serves 6

TO PREPARE AHEAD
Cook to the end of step 3 up to 12 hours ahead, but bake for only 20 minutes. Cover and store in the fridge for up to 12 hours. Sprinkle with a little more demerara sugar, then reheat in a preheated oven at 200°C/ Fan 180°C/Gas 6 for about 10–15 minutes, or until tender. Not suitable for freezing.

TO COOK IN THE AGA
Bake on the top set of runners in the Roasting Oven for about 15 minutes, or until tender.

Serves 6

TO PREPARE AHEAD
These can be made and kept in the fridge for up to 2 days ahead. Not suitable for freezing.

TO COOK IN THE AGA
Melt the two chocolates in separate bowls or jugs on the back of the Aga, stirring occasionally.

Ebony and Ivory Chocolate Pots

These look stunning made in small glasses (shot glasses are ideal) but of course you can use small ramekins or demi-tasse coffee cups if preferred. It is very rich so serve in very small portions. If you have Pyrex measuring jugs, melt the chocolate in these, which saves having to transfer the melted chocolate from the bowls for pouring into the glasses.

150g (5oz) 100% Belgian or
   Continental white chocolate
300ml (10 fl oz) single cream

150g (5oz) plain chocolate
about 6 large strawberries, sliced
   into quarters

1 Break the white chocolate into a heatproof bowl and pour over 150ml (5 fl oz) of the single cream.
2 Sit the bowl over a saucepan of hot water, ensure that it is not touching the water, and melt the chocolate over a low heat until smooth, stirring occasionally (make sure the chocolate does not get hot, otherwise it will go grainy). Pour into a jug.
3 In a separate heatproof bowl, repeat the process with the plain chocolate and remaining single cream. Melt until smooth. Pour into another jug.
4 Arrange 6 small glasses in front of you and, with a jug in each hand, pour both chocolates into each glass at the same time. This means that you get a different-coloured chocolate each side of the glass with a ripple effect in the middle. Leave 2.5cm (1 in) or so at the top of the glass for the strawberries.
5 Transfer to the fridge to set for a minimum of 1 hour.
6 About 15 minutes before serving, remove from the fridge. Arrange the strawberry quarters on top.

Raspberries with Mascarpone in a Chocolate Crust

A delicious tart to serve on a summer's evening, with the bonus that it can be prepared well in advance.

BISCUIT BASE
100g (4 oz) plain chocolate
225g (8 oz) milk chocolate
  Hobnob biscuits

FILLING
250g (9 oz) mascarpone cheese
1 x 200ml carton full-fat crème
  fraîche

1 teaspoon vanilla extract
caster sugar, to taste

TOPPING
500g (1 lb 2 oz) raspberries
4 tablespoons redcurrant jelly
1 tablespoon water

You will need a 23cm (9 in) springform tin, at least 5cm (2 in) deep.

1 Wet the inside of the tin and line the sides and base with a double layer of clingfilm.

2 First make the biscuit base. Melt the chocolate in a small bowl over a small pan of barely simmering water until just runny. Put the biscuits in a polythene bag and use a rolling pin to crush finely. Then add to the melted chocolate and mix together until blended. Using the back of a spoon, press the biscuit into the lined tin to cover the base and about 5cm (2 in) deep up the sides. Make sure the top edge is neat, then transfer to the fridge to set until firm.

3 Next make the filling. Mix together the mascarpone, crème fraîche, vanilla and caster sugar until smooth. Remove the chocolate case from the tin and peel away the clingfilm. Transfer to a serving platter.

4 Spread the filling over the base of the case. Arrange the raspberries on top, rounded side uppermost. Heat the redcurrant jelly and water in a small saucepan until melted. Leave to cool a little, then brush the raspberries with the glaze. Decorate with raspberry leaves if available. Before serving, bring to room temperature for about 20 minutes, it makes it easier to cut.

Serves 8

TO PREPARE AHEAD
Make the chocolate case up to a day ahead to the end of step 3. Fill on the day up to 12 hours ahead. Not suitable for freezing.

TO COOK IN THE AGA
Melt the chocolate in a bowl on the back or side of the Aga until just melted (no need to melt over a pan of simmering water – the heat of the Aga will melt the chocolate).

**Make up to 1 month ahead
and freeze.**

Boozy Orange Ice Cream

*No fuss, no need for an ice-cream machine, and no rewhisking
mid-freezing. This recipe is dead simple so long as you have an
electric whisk.*

4 oranges
4 large eggs, separated
150g (5 oz) caster sugar
*175ml (6 fl oz) orange juice, from
  a carton*

*85ml (3 fl oz) Cointreau or
  orange liqueur*
*300ml (10 fl oz) pouring double
  cream, lightly whipped*

1 Finely grate the zest from the oranges, and set aside. Cut away the
pith, and divide the oranges into segments. Keep in a covered bowl in
the fridge until ready to serve the ice cream.

2 To make the ice cream, put the egg whites in a clean bowl and whisk
on maximum speed until stiff and like a cloud. Gradually, 1 teaspoon at
a time, add all but 2 tablespoons of the sugar, whisking on maximum
speed until shiny and stiff.

3 In a large separate bowl, beat the egg yolks with the remaining
2 tablespoons of sugar until smooth and blended.

4 Heat the orange juice in a pan over a low heat to just simmering
point. Pour on to the egg yolks and mix to blend. Add the grated
orange zest. Return the mixture to the pan and heat gently, stirring
continuously with a wooden spoon, until it has thickened and the froth
has disappeared. Stir in the Cointreau.

5 Pour the custard back into the bowl, and carefully fold in the whisked
egg whites until smooth. Fold in the whipped cream.

6 Pour into a 500ml (18 fl oz) freezer-proof container, cover with a lid
and transfer to the freezer.

7 To serve, remove from the freezer about 20–30 minutes beforehand,
and serve spoonfuls with the orange segments.

Apricot and Pistachio Pavlova

Serves 6–8

A pavlova is spectacular, lovely for a buffet or a special supper party. No sugar is needed with the apricots as the meringue is very sweet. It is served with an apricot coulis, which you can make extra special by adding a little brandy.

3 large egg whites

175g (6 oz) caster sugar

1 teaspoon white wine vinegar

1 level teaspoon cornflour

FILLING

225g (8 oz) dried, ready-to-eat
  apricots

2 strips lemon zest

300ml (10 fl oz) double cream,
  whipped

50g (2 oz) pistachio nuts, roughly
  chopped

Preheat the oven to 160°C/Fan 140°C/Gas 3. Lay a piece of non-stick baking paper on a baking sheet and draw a 20cm (8 in) circle on it.

1 Put the egg whites in a clean bowl and whisk on the fastest speed with an electric whisk or in a free-standing mixer until stiff. Gradually, still whisking on maximum speed, add generous teaspoons of the sugar one at a time until the meringue is stiff and shiny and stands in peaks.

2 In a cup, blend together the vinegar and cornflour, and mix until smooth. Stir into the meringue.

3 Spread the meringue on to the paper, covering the circle, and build up the sides so they are higher than the centre to create a large nest.

4 Slide into the middle of the preheated oven, turn the heat down to 150°C/Fan 130°C/Gas 2, and bake for about 1 hour, or until the pavlova easily comes off the paper. It will be a pale creamy colour rather than white. Turn off the oven and leave the meringue undisturbed in the oven for about a further 1 hour to become cold.

5 For the filling, put the apricots into a pan with the lemon zest and just cover with cold water. Cover with a lid, bring to the boil and simmer

TO PREPARE AHEAD
Make the pavlova case up to 1 month ahead and keep wrapped in a cool place, or freeze for up to 2 months. The apricot purée and coulis can be made a day ahead.

TO COOK IN THE AGA
To cook the pavlova, slide on to the grid shelf on the floor of the Roasting Oven for about 3–4 minutes. Transfer to the Simmering Oven for about 1–1½ hours, or until easy to remove from the paper. To dry out, sit on a tea-towel on top of the flat lid of the Simmering Plate.

for about 10 minutes, or until soft. Carefully drain the apricots from the juice with a slotted spoon, reserving the juice, and put into a processor. Whizz until the fruit forms a smooth purée. If you do not have a processor, chop the apricots very finely and pass through a sieve. Tip into a bowl to cool.

6 Divide the apricot purée into 2 portions, using half for the coulis. Spoon into a bowl and dilute with the reserved juice until it reaches a sauce consistency.

7 Fold the remaining apricot purée into the cream, creating a marbled effect. Pile the cream in the centre of the pavlova and sprinkle with chopped pistachios.

8 Serve the pavlova in wedges with a spoonful of the apricot coulis.

Tea for a Crowd

Baking is one of my passions, as many of you will know. Bread baking, for instance, I find very therapeutic and relaxing, just the job for calming stress levels. Although I haven't actually included a bread recipe here, there are some tempting ideas for sandwiches and rolls (ideal for taking on a picnic tea), for scones, biscuits and cakes – some of them my familiar traybakes, which are so easy to bring together and bake. For stress-free preparation for a large celebratory tea – when you might have invited a load of people – never forget that a lot of baked goods, including (uniced) cakes, can be made well in advance and frozen. (The Aga might have been made for those who like baking at home.) Some muffins or scones might need to be oven-refreshed after thawing, but that won't be too demanding of your time, or too stressful.

Herb and Parmesan Soft Rolls

This is a quick and easy way of making rolls, either by hand or using a dough hook, which will save time and effort. This recipe will also make two small 450g (1 lb) loaves, but naturally they will take a little longer to bake. I have suggested leaving the dough to rise slowly overnight, which I find easier – I take it out of the fridge first thing and make the rolls later. If you prefer, leave to rise at room temperature to double its bulk.

450g (1 lb) strong white flour,
  plus extra for kneading
4 tablespoons olive oil, plus extra
  for glazing
350–450ml (12–15 fl oz) warm
  water
3 teaspoons salt
1 x 7g packet fast-action yeast

50g (2 oz) Parmesan, grated,
  plus extra for sprinkling
25g (1 oz) fresh chives, snipped
a good handful of fresh basil
  leaves, chopped
a good handful of fresh parsley,
  chopped
sunflower seeds

1 Measure the flour, oil, water, salt and yeast into the processor and mix, using the dough hook, for 5–8 minutes or until combined – the mixture will look quite wet – or mix by hand. Put into a large oiled bowl covered with clingfilm. Leave in the fridge overnight.

2 The next day, take the dough out of the fridge. It should have doubled in bulk. Leave the dough on one side for 1 hour to bring back to room temperature, then knock back by kneading in the mixer or by hand on a floured surface for 5 minutes.

3 Add the cheese and herbs, and continue to knead until they are well incorporated. Divide the dough into 20 pieces and roll into balls. Place close together on a greased baking sheet, and cover with an oiled plastic bag. (A cleaners' suit plastic bag is ideal – just tie a knot in the plastic where the hanger hole is.) Leave to prove in a warm place for about 30 minutes, or until the rolls have doubled in size.

Preheat the oven to 200°C/Fan 180°C/Gas 6.

4 Lightly glaze the rolls with oil, and sprinkle with sunflower seeds and the extra Parmesan. Bake in the centre of the preheated oven for about 20–25 minutes, or until the rolls are well risen, golden and sound hollow when tapped on the base. Best served warm.

Makes 20 rolls

TO PREPARE AHEAD
Complete step 1 the day before. Alternatively, the rolls can be baked the day before they are needed and then refreshed in a moderate oven at 180°C/Fan 160°C/Gas 4 for 15 minutes when required. To freeze, cool the cooked rolls completely, pack into a plastic bag and freeze for up to 3 months.

TO COOK IN THE AGA
Bake the rolls for about 20–30 minutes on the grid shelf on the floor of the Roasting Oven. Check after 15 minutes. To brown the bases, remove the grid shelf and put the baking sheet directly on the floor of the Roasting Oven.

Chicken liver pâté and snipped sun-blushed tomatoes

Pastrami, horseradish and lamb's lettuce

Tuna, mayonnaise, diced celery and watercress

Brie, halved seedless grapes and cranberry sauce

Hummus, roasted red peppers (from a jar in oil) and rocket

Grated mature Cheddar, beetroot and romaine lettuce

Ham and cucumber with mustard mayonnaise

Crispy bacon, mozzarella cheese and basil

Prawn, tartare sauce, spring onions and avocado (dip the avocado in lemon juice if making ahead)

Crab, curried mayonnaise and cucumber

Chicken, basil pesto and cherry tomatoes

Olive tapenade, sun-blushed tomatoes and Cambozola cheese

Prepare-Ahead Sandwiches

For lunch serve two rounds per person and for tea serve one and a half – less, if not for a hungry crowd. Serve two options of meat or fish and one vegetarian. These sandwiches can be made up to 2 days ahead, as below, complete with the fillings.

Start with really fresh bread. Buy thin- or medium-sliced bread, white or brown. Eighteen slices (9 rounds) makes about 36 sandwiches by cutting each round into 4 small sandwiches. Remember to season well and to use soft butter for flavour rather than a spread.

Fill the sandwiches, leaving the crusts on. Layer 4 sandwiches on top of each other on a large tray that will fit in your fridge. Cover with a layer of damp kitchen paper, then wrap tightly with clingfilm, and keep the tray in the fridge.

On the day of serving, remove the crusts from the sandwiches and cut into 4 (either triangles or rectangles). Ideally do this about 2 hours before eating. Cover with clingfilm, and keep at room temperature until serving.

SMOKED SALMON
1 loaf medium-sliced brown bread
100g (4 oz) butter, at room temperature
1 x 400g packet smoked salmon slices
salt and freshly ground black pepper
lemon wedges, to garnish

CREAM CHEESE, ROCKET AND MANGO CHUTNEY
1 loaf medium-sliced white bread
100g (4 oz) butter, at room temperature
225g (8 oz) full-fat cream cheese
½ x 360g jar spreadable mango chutney

1 x 50g bag rocket, roughly chopped
salt and freshly ground black pepper

EGG MAYONNAISE AND CHIVES
1 loaf medium-sliced white bread
100g (4 oz) butter, at room temperature
9 eggs, hard-boiled, chopped
about 150ml (5 fl oz) 'light', low-calorie mayonnaise
salt and freshly ground black pepper
1 large bunch fresh chives, snipped

Fresh Raspberry Scones

Makes about 12 small scones

Fresh blueberries can replace the raspberries if wished, but we prefer the raspberries! The scone dough is very deep to cut out once layered with the raspberries, so flour the cutter well between each cutting to prevent the dough sticking. Although the scones need to be eaten fresh, they also freeze extremely well.

The large scone made from the trimmings is perfect sliced for the family.

450g (1 lb) self-raising flour
4 level teaspoons baking powder
100g (4 oz) softened butter
50g (2 oz) caster sugar

2 large eggs
a little milk
about 100g (4 oz) fresh
  raspberries

Preheat the oven to 220°C/Fan 200°C/Gas 7. Lightly grease 2 baking sheets.

1 Measure the flour and baking powder into a large bowl. Add the butter and rub in with the fingertips until the mixture resembles fine breadcrumbs. Stir in the sugar.

2 Break the eggs into a measuring jug, then make up to 200ml (7 fl oz) with milk. Stir the egg and milk mixture into the flour – you may not need it all – and mix to a soft but not sticky dough.

3 Turn out on to a lightly floured work surface, knead lightly and then roll out to a rectangle about 2cm (¾ in) thick. Cut the rectangle of dough into 2 equal pieces.

4 Scatter the fresh raspberries evenly over 1 piece of dough. Top with the second rectangle of dough. Cut into as many rounds as possible with a fluted 5cm (2 in) cutter, and place on the prepared baking sheets. Gently push the trimmings together to form 1 large scone, and score the top with a sharp knife. Brush the tops of the scones with a little extra milk, or any egg and milk left in the jug.

5 Bake in the preheated oven for about 15 minutes, or until the scones are well risen and a pale golden brown. (The large scone will need about a further 5 minutes.) Cool on a wire rack. Eat as fresh as possible.

TO PREPARE AHEAD

Best eaten on the day of making. If you must, store in the fridge for 1 day once cooked. To serve, refresh in a preheated oven at 180°C/Fan 160°C/Gas 4 for about 10 minutes. Freeze the cooled scones in plastic bags for up to 6 months. Thaw, still in the bags, for 2–3 hours at room temperature and reheat to serve.

TO COOK IN THE AGA

Cook on the grid shelf on the lowest set of runners of the Roasting Oven for about 10–15 minutes.

Orange Chocolate Shortbread Biscuits

A variation on an old classic, and very easy to make. The chocolate becomes crisp and crunchy.

175g (6 oz) softened butter
75g (3 oz) caster sugar
175g (6 oz) plain flour
75g (3 oz) cornflour or semolina

1 x 85g bar Terry's chocolate orange, chopped into small pieces

Preheat the oven to 190°C/Fan 170°C/Gas 5. Lightly grease 2 baking sheets.

1 Measure the butter and sugar into a processor and process until soft. Add the flour and cornflour or semolina, and process until beginning to form coarse breadcrumbs. Scrape down the sides, remove the blade and stir in the chocolate pieces. If you do not have a processor, measure into a bowl and crumble with your fingertips to form coarse breadcrumbs.

2 Shape the mixture into 20 even-sized balls and put on to the prepared baking sheets. Flatten each ball with a fork. Bake in the preheated oven for about 15–20 minutes, or until the edges of the biscuits are golden. Allow to cool for 2–3 minutes, then transfer to a wire rack and leave until cold.

From left: Mega Chocolate Cookies (see page 172); Orange Chocolate Shortbread Biscuits; Frangipane Mince Pies (see page 166)

Makes 20 biscuits

TO PREPARE AHEAD
Bake, cool and store the biscuits in an airtight container for up to 1 week. Freeze the cooked biscuits in a rigid freezer-proof container for up to 2 months.

TO COOK IN THE AGA
2-oven Aga: Bake on the grid shelf sheet on the floor of the Roasting Oven for about 8 minutes, or until just pale golden at the edges. Watch carefully, if necessary sliding the cold sheet on the second set of runners above the biscuits to prevent further browning. Transfer to the Simmering Oven for a further 30–35 minutes, or until the biscuits are cooked through.

3- or 4-oven Aga: Bake on the grid shelf on the floor of the Baking Oven for about 15 minutes, or until just pale golden at the edges. Watch carefully, if necessary sliding the cold sheet on the second set of runners above the biscuits to prevent further browning. Transfer to the Simmering Oven for a further 30–35 minutes, or until the biscuits are cooked through.

TO PREPARE AHEAD

The chocolate cake will keep for 3 days in the fridge, but the icing will lose its shine. The lemon loaf and buns will also keep for 3 days. All will freeze well for up to 2 months, but uniced.

TO COOK IN THE AGA

2-oven Aga: Cook the cakes one after the other, starting with the buns, followed by the chocolate cake and then the loaf, on the grid shelf or floor of the Roasting Oven with the cold shelf on the second set of runners. The buns will take about 15–20 minutes, the chocolate cake about 20 minutes, the drizzle loaf about 30 minutes.

3- or 4-oven Aga: Cook on the grid shelf on the floor of the Baking Oven without the cold shelf for roughly the same timings as above.

Fast Baking – Make Three Cakes in One Go

On a recent TV programme I was asked to make 3 completely different types of cake from one basic cake mix: a superb chocolate cake, a lemon drizzle loaf and a dozen almond fruity buns. It's such a good and time-saving idea, especially when you have several friends to visit, perhaps over the weekend. If your oven is large, you can bake the cakes at the same time, or, if not, bake them in batches. One useful thing to know: modern baking powders are slower to react once the mix is made and put in the tin, so don't worry if it is an hour or so before the prepared cakes get put in the oven.

BASIC CAKE MIX	*350g (12 oz) caster sugar*
6 large eggs	*350g (12 oz) softened butter*
350g (12 oz) self-raising flour	*3 level teaspoons baking powder*

Preheat the oven to 180°C/Fan 160°C/Gas 4 for all the cakes.

1 Beat together all the ingredients until smooth in a large mixing bowl.
2 Divide the cake mix into two. Use one portion for the chocolate cake. Divide the remaining portion again into two, using one portion each for the lemon drizzle loaf and one for the almond fruity buns.

Top layer, left to right: Almond Fruity Buns; Chocolate Cake; Lemon Drizzle Loaf

Chocolate Cake with Wicked Chocolate Ganache Icing

40g (1½ oz) cocoa powder
4 tablespoons boiling water
half the basic cake mix
a little icing sugar, to serve

FOR SPREADING AND ICING
150ml (5 fl oz) double cream
150g (5 oz) plain chocolate,
   broken into pieces
4 tablespoons apricot jam

You will need 2 x 17cm (7 in) deep sandwich tins, greased and lined with non-stick baking paper.

1 Put the cocoa in a mixing bowl, and add the water a little at a time to make a stiff paste. Add to the cake mixture.

2 Turn into the prepared tins, level the top and bake in the preheated oven for about 20–25 minutes, or until shrinking away from the sides of the tin and springy to the touch.

3 Leave to cool in the tin, then turn on to a wire rack to become completely cold before icing.

4 To make the icing, measure the cream and chocolate into a bowl and carefully melt over a pan of hot water over a low heat, or gently in the microwave for 1 minute (600w microwave). Stir until melted, then set aside to cool a little and to thicken up.

5 To ice the cake, spread the apricot jam on the top of each cake. Spread half of the ganache icing on the top of the jam on one of the cakes, then lay the other cake on top, sandwiching them together. Use the remaining ganache icing to ice the top of the cake in a swirl pattern. Dust with icing sugar to serve.

Lemon Drizzle Loaf

Cuts into 6

finely grated zest of ½ lemon
half the remaining basic cake
  mix (a quarter of the original)

LEMON CRUNCHY ICING
50g (2 oz) granulated sugar
juice of ½ lemon

You will need a 450g (1 lb) loaf tin, greased and lined.

1 Add the lemon zest to the basic cake mix, and turn into the prepared tin.
2 Bake in the preheated oven for about 35 minutes, or until golden brown, shrinking away from the sides of the tin and springy to the touch.
3 While the cake is still warm, make the topping. Mix together the sugar and lemon juice, and pour over the warm cake.
4 Leave to cool a little and loosen the sides of the cake, then lift the cake out of the tin.

Almond Fruity Buns

Makes 12

50g (2 oz) sultanas
50g (2 oz) dried apricots, snipped
  into small pieces
25g (1 oz) ground almonds
the remaining quarter of the
  basic cake mix

TOPPING
a few flaked almonds

You will need a 12-hole bun tin, lined with paper cases.

1 Add the sultanas, apricots and ground almonds to the cake mix and stir until well mixed.
2 Turn into the prepared paper cases and sprinkle with the flaked almonds.
3 Bake in the preheated oven for about 20 minutes, or until golden brown and springy to the touch.

Complete to the end of step 4 up to 3 days ahead. Freeze the mince pies at the end of step 4 for up to 2 months.

Bake directly on the floor of the Roasting Oven for 8 minutes to brown the pastry base. Turn this round and slide on the grid shelf on the floor of the Roasting Oven for a further 6–8 minutes until well risen and golden brown. You may need the cold sheet on the second set of runners if getting too brown.

Frangipane Mince Pies

If you want to make a large tart you can use the exact quantity below to fill a 23cm (9 in) loose-bottomed flan tin which will take about 25 minutes in the preheated oven. These mince pies are best served warm. (See photo on page 160.)

PASTRY	2 large eggs
225g (8 oz) plain flour	*100g (4 oz) ground almonds*
100g (4 oz) butter, cut into cubes	*15g (½ oz) plain flour*
25g (1 oz) icing sugar	*½ teaspoon almond extract,*
1 egg, beaten	*or to taste*

FRANGIPANE	FILLING
100g (4 oz) softened butter	*just under 1 x 410g jar*
100g (4 oz) caster sugar	*mincemeat*

Preheat the oven to 200°C/Fan 180°C / Gas 6. You will need deep mince pie tins for 24 pies and a 6.5cm (2½ in) cutter.

1 To make the pastry, measure the flour, butter and icing sugar into a food processor bowl, then process until the mixture resembles breadcrumbs. Pour in the beaten egg and pulse the blade until the dough starts to form a ball. Knead lightly, wrap and chill for about 30 minutes.

2 To make the frangipane, measure the butter and sugar into the unwashed processor, and blend until soft and creamy. Scrape down the sides, add the eggs and continue to process. Don't worry if the mixture looks curdled at this stage. Add the ground almonds, flour and almond extract, and mix briefly.

3 Roll the pastry out thinly on a lightly floured work surface and line the tins. Spoon a teaspoonful of mincemeat into each tartlet and top with the frangipane mixture. Do not over fill the tins.

4 Bake in the preheated oven for about 15–17 minutes, watching carefully. Remove from the tins and allow to cool a little on a wire rack.

Lemon Yoghurt Cake

A really moist plain cake, which is best eaten within the week. Like a Madeira cake, it doesn't need icing. This amount of mixture fills 2 x 450g (1 lb) loaf tins. Don't attempt to cook it in one large 900g (2 lb) loaf tin as it is apt to burn, being in the oven for a longer time.

75g (3 oz) butter, at room
  temperature
300g (10 oz) caster sugar
3 large eggs, separated

grated zest of 1 lemon
1 x 200ml carton Greek yoghurt
225g (8 oz) self-raising flour

Preheat the oven to 180°C/Fan 160°C/Gas 4. You will need 2 x 450g (1 lb) loaf tins (top measurement 17 x 11cm/7 x 4 in).

1 Grease and line the tins with a long strip of greased greaseproof paper also covering the two long sides of the tin.
2 In a bowl, cream together the butter and sugar, using an electric whisk, until thoroughly blended. Add the egg yolks and lemon zest, blend well, then add the yoghurt. Mix until smooth, then fold in the flour.
3 In a separate bowl, whisk the egg whites with the electric whisk until stiff but not dry, and fold carefully into the cake mixture. Divide the mixture between the 2 tins, and gently level the surface.
4 Bake in the preheated oven for 35–40 minutes, or until well risen, golden and firm to the touch.
5 To test whether the cake is done, insert a skewer. When it comes out clean with no uncooked mixture sticking to it, it is done. Turn the cakes out and allow to cool on a wire rack.

Makes 2 loaf cakes

TO PREPARE AHEAD
The cakes will keep for up to 1 week, stored in an airtight container in a cool place. Wrap and freeze the cake at the end of step 5 for up to 2 months. Thaw for about 4 hours at room temperature.

TO COOK IN THE AGA
2-oven Aga: Bake on the grid shelf on the floor of the Roasting Oven with the cold plain shelf on the second set of runners for about 35 minutes. If the cakes are becoming too dark, cover loosely with foil.

3- or 4-oven Aga: Bake on the grid shelf on the floor of the Baking Oven for about 35 minutes.

Cuts into 8–10 wedges

TO PREPARE AHEAD

Make the cakes and store in an airtight container for up to 3 days before filling and icing. Make the filling/icing on the day you serve the cake. Wrap and freeze the uniced cake for up to 3 months. Thaw for about 4 hours at room temperature, then fill and ice.

TO COOK IN THE AGA

2 oven-Aga: Bake on the grid shelf on the floor of the Roasting Oven with the cold shelf on the second set of runners for about 25 minutes. Turn halfway through baking.

3- or 4-oven Aga: Bake on the grid shelf on the floor of the Baking Oven for 25 minutes, sliding in the cold shelf on the second set of runners only if the cakes become too dark.

Ginger and Orange Cake with Mascarpone Icing

A delicious and light cake, best kept in the fridge because of the icing. It is a true favourite with all who work with me!

225g (8 oz) self-raising flour
2 level teaspoons baking powder
225g (8 oz) softened butter
225g (8 oz) caster sugar
4 large eggs

5–6 bulbs stem ginger in syrup, coarsely chopped, plus syrup
finely grated zest of 1 orange
1 x 250g carton full-fat mascarpone cheese

Preheat the oven to 180°C/Fan 160°C/Gas 4. Grease well and line the base of 2 x 20cm (8 in) deep sandwich tins with non-stick baking paper.

1 In a large mixing bowl, mix together the flour, baking powder, butter, sugar, eggs, 3–4 bulbs of the ginger and the orange zest, using an electric mixer, until thoroughly blended. Divide the mixture evenly between the prepared tins and level out.

2 Bake in the centre of the preheated oven for 20–25 minutes, or until golden brown and shrinking away from the sides of the tin. Leave to cool for a few moments, then turn out on to a wire rack to cool.

3 For the filling/icing, beat the mascarpone with 2 tablespoons of the ginger syrup. When the cakes are completely cold, sandwich with half of this mixture. Spread the remainder on top of the cake and sprinkle over the remaining coarsely chopped ginger.

Wicked Chocolate Brownies

These are expensive to make, but worth it, and are even better when kept for 2–3 days. As with all chocolate brownies, expect the mixture to sink slightly after baking.

300g (10 oz) soft butter,
375g (13 oz) caster sugar
4 large eggs
1 teaspoon baking powder

75g (3 oz) cocoa powder
100g (4 oz) plain flour
1 x 100g (4 oz) packet of plain
 chocolate 'polka dots'

Preheat the oven to 180°C/Fan 160°C/Gas 4. You will need a traybake tin 30 x 23cm (12 x 9 in) or a small roasting tin, lined with foil and well greased.

1 In a bowl, mix together all the ingredients until well blended. This can also be done in a processor, mixing in the 'polka dots' by hand at the last minute. Spoon the mixture into the prepared tin and level the top.
2 Bake in the preheated oven for 35–40 minutes, or until shrinking away from the edge of the tin.
3 Cool in the tin. When cold, remove the foil. Store wrapped in clean foil, or in a cake tin in the larder. Cut into squares to serve.

Makes about 32 pieces

TO PREPARE AHEAD
Make ahead, cool, cut into squares and keep in an airtight container for up to 1 week. Pack and freeze the cake whole when completely cold for up to 6 months.

TO COOK IN THE AGA
2-oven Aga: Put the tin on the grid shelf on the floor of the Roasting Oven with the cold plain shelf above on the second set of runners, and bake for about 25 minutes until set. Then very carefully transfer the now-hot plain shelf to the middle of the Simmering Oven and bake for about a further 20 minutes, or until a skewer comes out clean when inserted into the centre.

3- or 4-oven Aga: Put the grid shelf on the floor of the Baking Oven, and bake for about 25 minutes, making sure that the top does not get too dark. If it does, slip the cold plain shelf above on the second set of runners for the last 5 minutes. Then transfer the roasting tin to the centre of the Simmering Oven for a further 20 minutes or so, or until a skewer comes out clean when inserted into the centre.

Norfolk Fruit Cake with Ginger

This easy cake is really moist – with the added bonus that this makes it keep well – and it is packed with fruits, including apricots and cherries. If you have no ginger in the store-cupboard, simply increase the amount of the other fruits to make up the weight. It is just as delectable even without the ginger.

450g (1 lb) mixed dried fruits and nuts, such as apricots, roughly chopped; glacé cherries, quartered; shelled nuts, roughly chopped; raisins, sultanas

100g (4 oz) soft butter

1 teaspoon bicarbonate of soda

175g (6 oz) light muscovado sugar

225ml (8 fl oz) water

2 large eggs, beaten

300g (10 oz) self-raising wholemeal flour

2 teaspoons ground ginger

100–175 (4–6 oz) stem ginger, drained of syrup, roughly chopped

Preheat the oven to 180°C/Fan 160°C/Gas 4. You will need a 20cm (8 in) deep round cake tin, greased and lined.

1 Measure the prepared fruits and nuts, butter or margarine, bicarbonate of soda, sugar and water into a large pan. Bring up to the boil, and boil for 3 minutes.

2 Allow to cool, then add the eggs, flour, ground ginger and stem ginger. Mix to thoroughly combine, then turn into the prepared tin and level the top.

3 Bake in the preheated oven for about 1¼ hours until golden brown.

4 Cool in the tin before turning out on to a wire rack.

Makes 1 cake – cuts into 8 pieces

TO PREPARE AHEAD
Cool completely, then wrap in greaseproof paper and foil and store in a cool place for up to 2 months. To freeze, put into a large freezer bag, and freeze for up to 3 months. Thaw for about 8 hours at room temperature.

TO COOK IN THE AGA
2-oven Aga: For step 3, stand the cake tin in the large roasting tin on the grid rack in the lowest position and hang on the lowest set of runners in the Roasting Oven, with the cold plain shelf on the second set of runners from the top. Cook for 30 minutes. If, after 20 minutes, it is getting a little brown at the sides, give it a gentle half-turn. Transfer the now-hot plain shelf to the centre of the Simmering Oven, place the cake on top for a further 1½ hours.

3- or 4-oven Aga: For step 3, bake the cake on the grid shelf on the floor of the Baking Oven for about 1¼ hours. Check after 30 minutes, and if the top is getting too brown, slide the cold plain shelf on the second set of runners from above to prevent further browning.

Makes 16

Mega Chocolate Cookies

TO PREPARE AHEAD
Make up to 2 days ahead, store in an airtight container and refresh in a preheated oven at 180°C/Fan 160°C/Gas 4 for 8–10 minutes. Cool to let them become crisp. To freeze, cool completely, store for up to 2 months.

TO COOK IN THE AGA
2-oven Aga: Cook on the grid shelf on the floor of the Roasting Oven with the cold shelf on the second set of runners for about 15–20 minutes, turning round after about 10 minutes. In the Aga the cookies will spread slightly more than in a conventional oven.

3- or 4-oven Aga: Cook on the grid shelf on the floor of the Baking Oven with the cold sheet on the second set of runners for about 15–20 minutes. If not quite brown enough, remove the cold sheet for the final 5 minutes.

For speed you can use chocolate chips or 'polka dots', but I like the large chunks of roughly chopped chocolate! These taste just as good if made normal size. (See photo on page 160.)

225g (8 oz) soft butter
175g (6 oz) caster sugar
100g (4 oz) light muscovado sugar
1 teaspoon vanilla extract

2 large eggs, beaten
300g (10 oz) self-raising flour
225g (8 oz) plain chocolate, cut into chunks

Preheat the oven to 190°C/Fan 170°C/Gas 5. Lightly grease 4 baking sheets.

1 In a large bowl, mix together the butter and sugars thoroughly until evenly blended. Add the vanilla extract to the eggs, then add these gradually to the mixture in the bowl, beating well between each addition. Next add the flour, mix in and lastly stir in the chocolate chunks.

2 Spoon large tablespoons of the mixture on to the prepared baking sheets, leaving room for the cookies to spread. (You will be able to fit only about 4 per sheet!)

3 Bake in the top of the preheated oven for about 15 minutes, or until just golden. Allow to cool on the sheet for 2–3 minutes before lifting off with a palette knife or fish slice. Allow to cool completely on a wire rack.

Divine Dark Chocolate Cake with White Chocolate and Orange Icing

An indulgent cake for special occasions. I tried making this with just self-raising flour rather than baking powder and bicarbonate of soda, and it was not so successful. The butter should be very soft, but not oily and melted.

CHOCOLATE CAKE
50g (2 oz) cocoa powder
200ml (7 fl oz) cold water
175g (6 oz) plain flour
¼ teaspoon baking powder
1 level teaspoon bicarbonate of
   soda
100g (4 oz) soft butter
300g (10 oz) caster sugar
3 large eggs

WHITE CHOCOLATE FILLING
AND ICING
225g (8 oz) Continental white
   chocolate, broken into small
   pieces
150ml (5 fl oz) double cream
finely grated zest of 1 small
   orange
1 x 100g carton full-fat
   Philadelphia cream cheese

Preheat the oven to 180°C/Fan 160°C/Gas 4. You will need 2 x 20cm (8in) round sandwich tins, greased and base-lined.

1 Begin with the icing because it needs to cool before use. Measure the chocolate and cream into a small bowl and sit it over a pan of just-hot water. Allow to melt, stirring occasionally until smooth. Add the orange zest. In a bowl, mash down the cream cheese and slowly beat in the white chocolate. Chill until it achieves a spreading consistency.

2 To make the cake, measure the cocoa into a mixing bowl, pour over the water, and whisk until it reaches a loose batter consistency. Add all the remaining cake ingredients and whisk or beat until just smooth. Do not overbeat.

3 Divide the mixture between the cake tins and bake in the preheated oven for about 25 minutes, or until well risen and shrinking away from the sides of the tins.

4 When the cakes are cold, sandwich together with half the chocolate icing. Spread the remaining icing on top. Alternatively, split each sponge in half and divide the icing into 4 portions. Fill the three layers with the icing and spread the remainder on top.

TO PREPARE AHEAD
The completed filled cake can be kept in the fridge for 1 week. Unfilled, the cake will freeze for up to 1 month.

TO COOK IN THE AGA
2-oven Aga: Bake on the grid shelf on the floor of the Roasting Oven with the cold plain shelf on the second set of runners for about 25–30 minutes.

3- or 4-oven Aga: Bake in the Baking Oven for the same time in the same position as above, but without the cold plain shelf.

TO PREPARE AHEAD
Can be made and kept in
the fridge for up to 2 days.
Freeze when cooked for up
to 2 months.

TO COOK IN THE AGA
Bake on the grid shelf on the
floor of the Roasting Oven for
about 20 minutes.

Apple and Cinnamon Muffins

*Great for breakfast or elevenses, these are best served warm. This
quick and easy recipe is a perfect way of using up apples that are
past their best in the fruit bowl.*

400g (14 oz) plain flour
1 tablespoon ground cinnamon
175g (6 oz) caster sugar
1 tablespoon baking powder
300ml (10 fl oz) milk
2 large eggs, beaten

175g (6 oz) butter, melted and
   cooled
2 dessert apples, peeled, cored
   and finely chopped
2 tablespoons demerara sugar

**Preheat the oven to 200°C/Fan 180°C/Gas 6. Line a 12-hole
muffin tin with paper cases.**

1 Measure the flour, cinnamon, caster sugar and baking powder into a
large mixing bowl, and stir until mixed evenly.
2 Measure the milk into a jug, add the eggs and stir in the melted
butter. Mix until combined.
3 Make a well in the centre of the dry ingredients and pour in the egg
mixture. Stir with a wooden spoon until evenly mixed, then stir in the
chopped apples.
4 Spoon the mixture evenly into the muffin cases so that it comes to the
top of the cases. Sprinkle with demerara sugar.
5 Bake in the preheated oven for about 25 minutes, or until the muffins
have risen and are golden brown on top.

Crunchy Iced Lemon Traybake

Cuts into about 24 pieces

This easy cake is delicious served warm or cold. When we were in Australia, we had a similar cake with poppy seeds (about 40g/1½ oz, added to the sponge mixture) which makes an unusual variation. It was always served warm, heated in a microwave.

300g (10 oz) self-raising flour

225g (8 oz) caster sugar

4 large eggs

225g (8 oz) softened butter

2 level teaspoons baking powder

finely grated zest of 2 lemons

4 tablespoons milk

TOPPING

225g (8 oz) granulated sugar

juice of 2 large juicy lemons

Preheat the oven to 180°C/Fan 160°C/Gas 4. You will need a traybake tin 30 x 23cm (12 x 9 in) or a small roasting tin, lined with foil, and well greased with extra margarine or butter.

1 Measure all of the cake ingredients into an electric mixer, processor or bowl and beat well until smooth. Turn the mixture into the prepared tin.
2 Bake in the preheated oven for 30–35 minutes, or until the cake is golden brown and coming away from the sides of the tin.
3 Remove the cake from the oven but do not turn out. Mix together the topping ingredients and pour over the surface of the hot cake. Leave in the tin until barely warm, then use the foil lining to lift out. When cold, cut into about 24 pieces.

TO PREPARE AHEAD

Best freshly made, although it will keep in an airtight container for 2–3 days. Freeze whole, well wrapped in foil, for about 2 months. Thaw at room temperature for 2–3 hours.

TO COOK IN THE AGA

2-oven Aga: Hang the small roasting tin on the lowest set of runners in the Roasting Oven and slide the cold plain shelf on the second set of runners. Bake for about 25 minutes, or until the cake is golden brown and coming away from the sides of the tin. Turn the tin round after 20 minutes if the baking is not even. (Double the recipe for the large roasting tin and bake for 30–35 minutes.)

3- or 4-oven Aga: Hang the roasting tin on the lowest set of runners in the Baking Oven. Should the cake become too brown after, say, 20 minutes, slide the cold plain shelf above it on the second set of runners.

To warm the cake for serving, use the Simmering Oven.

Buffets

I love giving big parties, and the most stress-free way of doing this is to offer a buffet: a hot or cold main course or two, with a selection of salads, as well as a choice of puddings, of course (and these you can choose from the Puddings and Desserts chapter). There are some interesting new ideas here, my favourite being the Malaysian Rice, which was a great success at a summer lunch party not long ago. Although there will be lots of planning and shopping to do, many of the dishes here can be prepared well in advance and frozen. Remember to allow enough time for thawing.

The recipes here are for ten people, but they can be doubled (or trebled) if you are really going to town with numbers. It may seem obvious, but do remember to have enough plates, knives, forks, spoons and glasses!

For more buffet ideas, see:

Bacon and Rocket Tart with Parmesan Pastry

This is a delicious tart, which is perfect when cooking for a crowd.

PARMESAN PASTRY
225g (8 oz) plain flour
1 teaspoon English mustard
  powder
50g (2 oz) butter
50g (2 oz) lard
50g (2 oz) Parmesan, grated
1 large egg, beaten
1–2 tablespoons water

FILLING
2 tablespoons olive oil
250g (9 oz) smoked bacon,
  chopped

2 large onions, finely sliced
250g (9 oz) chestnut mushrooms,
  sliced
salt and freshly ground black
  pepper
100g (4 oz) Gruyère cheese,
  grated
100g (4 oz) rocket, roughly
  chopped
4 large eggs
1 x 200ml carton full-fat crème
  fraîche
300ml (10 fl oz) double cream
100g (4 oz) Parmesan, grated

Serves 10

TO PREPARE AHEAD
At the end of step 5, cool quickly, cover and keep in the fridge up to 48 hours ahead. Reheat to serve. At the end of step 5, cool quickly, wrap and freeze for up to 1 month.

TO COOK IN THE AGA
There is no need to bake blind in the Aga. Spoon the filling into the raw pastry case and slide directly on to the floor of the Roasting Oven and bake for about 40 minutes, or until golden brown and the pastry is crisp.

Preheat the oven to 180°C/Fan 160°C/Gas 4. You will need a 28cm (11 in) deep, loose-bottomed, round flan tin.

1 First make the pastry. Measure the flour, mustard, butter and lard into a processor or a bowl, and process or rub in until the mixture resembles fine breadcrumbs. Add the Parmesan, egg and water, and mix again just as long as it takes for the ingredients to come together.

2 Roll the pastry thinly on a lightly floured work surface, then carefully use to line the flan tin. Prick the base, then chill for 30 minutes. Place a sheet of greaseproof paper in the tart case and fill with baking beans or rice. Bake blind in the preheated oven for about 15 minutes, or until the sides are pale golden. Remove the baking beans and paper, and return to the hot oven to bake for another 10 minutes, or until the base of the case is cooked and crispy.

3 Next make the filling. Heat the oil in a large non-stick frying pan. Add the bacon and fry for 2–3 minutes, then add the onion. Cover and cook gently over a low heat until the onions are soft and the bacon is cooked.

Remove the lid and continue to cook to drive off any liquid. Then add the mushrooms and fry until just cooked. Season, remove from the heat and set aside to cool.

4 Spoon the cooled mixture into the flan case, then sprinkle over the Gruyère cheese and rocket. Beat together the eggs, crème fraîche and cream, and add seasoning. Pour the custard over the mushrooms and bacon. Sprinkle over the Parmesan.

5 Place the tart on a baking sheet and carefully slide into the preheated oven. Cook for 35–40 minutes, or until the filling is just set and the top is golden brown.

Grainy Mustard and Herb Potato Salad

Potato salad is always a favourite for a buffet. This is a delicious variation with a slightly lighter dressing.

1.5kg (3 lb 5 oz) baby new
  potatoes, scrubbed
1 large mild onion, thinly sliced
salt and freshly ground black
  pepper
8 tablespoons 'light', low-calorie
  mayonnaise
3 tablespoons snipped fresh
  chives

2 tablespoons chopped fresh
  parsley

VINAIGRETTE
2 tablespoons grainy mustard
3 tablespoons white wine vinegar
2 tablespoons lemon juice
2 teaspoons caster sugar
8 tablespoons olive oil

1 Slice the new potatoes in half lengthways. Boil with the onion in salted water for about 15 minutes, or until just tender. Drain and set aside to cool for no more than 5 minutes.

2 While the potatoes and onions are cooking, make the vinaigrette. In a bowl, mix together all the ingredients and whisk by hand to blend. Season well.

3 When the potatoes and onion have cooled but are still warm, pour over the vinaigrette, stir gently and set aside until cold.

4 In a small bowl, mix together the mayonnaise and herbs, and combine with the cold potatoes. Serve at room temperature.

Serves 10 with other salads

TO PREPARE AHEAD
Complete to the end of step 3 up to 48 hours ahead. In step 4, the mayonnaise and herbs can be mixed up to 48 hours in advance but do not combine with the potatoes until about 10 hours ahead. Not suitable for freezing.

Three Bean, Tomato and Asparagus Salad

This can be made ahead completely as the beans can marinate in the dressing and the tomatoes will not lose too much liquid. Serve on a stylish platter for the buffet table, preferably a long narrow one.

1 x 400g can lentils
1 x 400g can flageolet beans
1 x 400g can black-eyed beans
4 spring onions, sliced on the
  diagonal
6 tablespoons good salad
  dressing
salt and freshly ground black
  pepper

225g (8 oz) asparagus tips
10 tomatoes, skinned and sliced
1 tablespoon balsamic vinegar
2 tablespoons olive oil
a handful of freshly snipped
  chives and torn fresh basil
  leaves

1 Drain and rinse the lentils and beans. Pat dry on kitchen paper, then mix together in a bowl. Stir in the spring onions, salad dressing and seasoning. Arrange down the centre of a thin flat dish.

2 Cook the asparagus tips in boiling salted water for about 3–4 minutes, or until just tender. Drain and refresh in cold water. Dry on kitchen paper.

3 Arrange the tomato slices over the beans, overlapping. Arrange the asparagus tips in a herringbone shape down the centre of the tomatoes. Season well.

4 Mix together the balsamic vinegar and oil, then drizzle over the whole dish. Sprinkle over the chives and basil, and serve.

Serves 10–12

TO PREPARE AHEAD
Make completely to the end of step 3 up to some 12 hours ahead. Not suitable for freezing.

Serves 10 with other salads

TO PREPARE AHEAD

Most of this salad can be made the day before – just add the chickpeas and dressing on the day so everything stays crisp. Not suitable for freezing.

Chickpea and Pesto Salad

This salad is Italian inspired, and is wonderful as an accompaniment to cold meats in the summer – or by itself for non-meat eaters. If preferred, replace the chickpeas with mixed beans, such as cannellini or flageolet.

2 small garlic cloves, crushed
2 x 400g cans chickpeas, rinsed and drained
100g (4 oz) mixed olives, pitted and quartered
225g (8 oz) feta cheese, cubed
225g (8 oz) sun-blushed tomatoes, roughly chopped
5 tablespoons chopped fresh parsley

DRESSING
4 tablespoons balsamic vinegar
4 tablespoons green pesto, bought or home-made
4 tablespoons olive oil
salt and freshly ground black pepper

1 Measure all the ingredients for the dressing into a large bowl, seasoning well, and whisk until combined.

2 Add the remaining ingredients to the dressing, toss and season well. Serve at room temperature.

Beetroot, Carrot and Sultana Salad

This salad looks very pretty, and its dressing has an unusual sweet and sour flavour. If you are making this in the summer, and have an abundance of herbs in the garden, add 2 tablespoons chopped fresh coriander or chives if liked.

SALAD
1kg (2¼ lb) cooked beetroot, finely diced
2 shallots, very finely chopped
2 large carrots, peeled and cut into 1cm (½ in) cubes
50g (2 oz) sultanas
salt and freshly ground black pepper

2 tablespoons chopped fresh parsley

DRESSING
3 tablespoons grainy mustard
3 tablespoons white wine vinegar
6 tablespoons olive oil
3 tablespoons runny honey

1 In a large bowl, mix together all the ingredients for the salad, except the parsley.

2 Measure the ingredients for the dressing into a bowl and whisk to combine.

3 Pour the dressing over the salad, season well and sprinkle with the parsley.

Serves 10 with other salads

TO PREPARE AHEAD
Cook the beetroot up to 4 days ahead and keep in the fridge but prepare everything else at the last minute. Not suitable for freezing.

TO PREPARE AHEAD
Complete up to the end of
step 3 the day before, but add
the cauliflower florets only
when reheating the dish.
Not suitable for freezing.

TO COOK IN THE AGA
For step 1, fry on the Boiling
Plate. Continue with step 2,
bring to the boil, cover and
transfer to the Simmering
Oven, and cook for about
15 minutes. At step 3, remove
the lid and continue to cook
on the Boiling Plate.

Creamy Vegetable Curry

*Unlike some curries, this is very quick to prepare and cook. It has
more of a Thai influence than an Indian. Alongside other curries
and rice, it could make a good meal for a non-meat eater.*

*2 tablespoons sunflower oil
2 large onions, roughly chopped
2 fresh red chillies, seeded and
   finely chopped
6cm (2½ in) piece fresh ginger
   root, peeled and finely grated
3–4 tablespoons medium curry
   powder
2 tablespoons ground turmeric
4 x 400g cans chopped tomatoes
1.1 litres (2 pints) chicken or
   vegetable stock*

*700g (1½ lb) carrots, cut into
   2.5cm (1 in) batons
700g (1½ lb) new potatoes,
   scrubbed and halved
   lengthways
700g (1½ lb) cauliflower,
   cut into small florets
2 x 200ml cartons or cans
   coconut cream
salt and freshly ground black
   pepper*

1 Heat the oil in a large, deep non-stick frying pan. Add the onion, chilli,
ginger and spices, and fry over a high heat for about 2–3 minutes.
2 Add the tomatoes and their juices, the stock, carrots and potatoes.
Cover with a lid, bring to the boil and simmer over a low heat for about
15 minutes or until the potatoes are just tender.
3 Remove the lid, and add the cauliflower florets and coconut cream.
Season well and boil for a further 5 minutes, uncovered, until all the
vegetables are cooked and the sauce has thickened.
4 Check the seasoning, and serve hot.

Spiced Honeyed Ham

This is equally good with smoked or unsmoked gammon, whether on or off the bone, whichever appeals to you most. If it is off the bone, the gammon will fit into a pan more easily. Check with your butcher whether the joint needs soaking as this will depend on the cure.

This recipe is an updated version of the hay box method that our great-grandmothers used. It is very 'green' because it means you don't need to simmer the joint for hours, which is not only costly but also difficult to control: if gammon is cooked too fast, it shrinks. If you prefer a more conventional method, simmer very slowly for about 3½ hours, leaving it to cool in the cooking liquids. If you have a meat thermometer, it should read 170°C when the gammon is done.

1 small gammon, about 6.3kg (14 lb)

GLAZE
about 100g (4 oz) demerara sugar

2 tablespoons runny honey
1 tablespoon dry English mustard
1 teaspoon mixed spice

You will need a really large deep pan with a lid, large enough to hold the gammon, ideally a preserving pan. (You may be able to borrow one from a local school.) You will also need a 'hay box'. In an undisturbed part of the kitchen, place on the floor a couple of old blankets, an old duvet or an opened out old sleeping bag. Protect this with a layer of opened old newspapers.

1 Soak the gammon in cold water for 24 hours (check first with your butcher; see above).
2 Lift the gammon into the deep pan and cover with water. Bring up to the boil, then simmer very gently for 1–1¼ hours. Then bring to a full rolling boil and transfer to your hay box.
3 Place the pan on top in the centre, cover with a lid and completely wrap it up as if in a cocoon. Do not disturb the pan or it will lose heat. Leave for minimum of 20 hours or until cooked.

Serves 10

TO PREPARE AHEAD
At the end of step 5, cool quickly, wrap and keep in the fridge 2 or 3 days ahead. Ham will keep in this way for up to 2 weeks. Not suitable for freezing.

TO COOK IN THE AGA
At step 2, cook in the Simmering Oven in a parcel of foil in the large roasting tin overnight, for about 14 hours. Check with a skewer pierced into the thickest part. The juices that flow should run clear. Continue from step 4 and brown in the Roasting Oven.

4 The next day, you will find that the pan is still hot. Lift out the ham from the liquid and drain. (When it is cooked, gammon is called ham!)

To brown the ham, preheat the oven to 220°C/Fan 200°C/Gas 7. Line a large roasting tin with foil.

5 Take the skin off the ham and discard. Mix together the glaze ingredients and spread over the ham. Score the skin with a knife, making a diagonal pattern. Lift the ham into the prepared roasting tin. Brown in the preheated oven for 10–20 minutes, watching like a hawk and turning once. Allow to get completely cold.

6 Serve cold with mustard and chutneys.

Five-Spice Mango Chicken

This is perfect to serve cold for a buffet or when cooking for numbers, as it is so light and fresh – and there is not a drop of mayonnaise in sight! It can be made a day ahead and kept in the fridge, which gives time for the flavours to really infuse into the chicken. It is also surprisingly good served hot (see step 4).

750g (1¾ lb) fresh cooked
  chicken meat, without bones

MANGO SAUCE
1 large mango, peeled
8 mild peppadew peppers, from
  a jar
6 tablespoons mango chutney
1 x 200ml carton Greek yoghurt
1 tablespoon Chinese five-spice
  powder

juice of 1 lemon
a few drops of Tabasco
salt and freshly ground black
  pepper

GARNISH
fresh salad leaves
2 mild peppadew peppers, from
  a jar, drained and thinly sliced
chopped fresh parsley

1 For the sauce, cut the flesh of half the mango roughly into pieces and put in a food processor. Add the rest of the ingredients, and whizz until smooth and blended. Season well.

2 Cut the chicken into neat pieces and mix with the mango sauce in a mixing bowl. Cut the flesh of the remaining half mango into 1cm (½ in) pieces and add to the chicken mixture. Stir to combine. Taste and check the seasoning.

3 To serve cold, spoon the chicken mixture into a dish, decorate with a few salad leaves, and sprinkle over the peppadew slices and parsley.

4 To serve hot, simply add 1 tablespoon cornflour to the mango mixture before blending in the processor. Then add the chicken and fresh mango, pile into a shallow ovenproof dish, and bake in a preheated oven at 200°C/Fan 180°C/Gas 6 for about 15 minutes, or until very hot. Sprinkle with peppadew slices and parsley, and serve.

Serves 10

TO PREPARE AHEAD

To serve cold, and to make a day ahead, do not add the chopped fresh mango at step 2. Mix the fruit with a little lemon juice and keep in a bowl in the fridge. At step 3, just stir in the mango before sprinkling over the peppadew slices and parsley, and serving. Not suitable for freezing.

TO COOK IN THE AGA

To serve hot, follow step 4 and slide the dish on to the second set of runners in the Roasting Oven and cook for about 15 minutes, or until very hot. Sprinkle with peppadew slices and parsley, and serve.

Chilled Gazpacho Chicken

Gazpacho is an old favourite cold soup for summer. I have combined the raw ingredients with cooked chicken to make an up-to-date Coronation Chicken. You can, of course, use cooked turkey instead of the chicken. When buying the black olives, the best kind come in olive oil from the deli counter.

2 medium chickens, cooked (yielding about 900g/2 lb meat)
200ml (7 fl oz) 'light', low-calorie mayonnaise
1 x 200ml carton full-fat crème fraîche
4 tablespoons sun-dried tomato paste
18–20 peppadew peppers, from a jar, drained and thinly sliced
2 garlic cloves, crushed
12 spring onions, white part only, thinly sliced
salt and freshly ground black pepper

4 teaspoons balsamic vinegar
4 tablespoons chopped fresh basil

GARNISH SALAD
2 small cucumbers, peeled, seeded and cubed
500g (1 lb 2 oz) cherry tomatoes, halved
100g (4 oz) black olives
chopped fresh parsley
a little French dressing
a handful basil leaves, to garnish

1 Cut the chicken into neat bite-sized pieces, removing all the skin and bone.
2 In a large bowl, mix together the mayonnaise and crème fraîche with the sun-dried tomato paste, peppers and garlic. Fold in the chicken pieces and spring onions, then taste and adjust the seasoning. Add the balsamic vinegar and basil.
3 Combine the cucumbers, tomatoes, olives and parsley in a bowl but don't add the vinaigrette until just before serving.
4 Spoon the chicken on to a flat serving dish. When ready to serve, add the vinaigrette to the salad. Garnish the chicken with the salad and the basil leaves.

The Perfect Whole Roast Fillet of Beef with Thyme

Cold rare roast fillet of beef is sheer luxury for a special occasion. So often a beautifully cooked fillet is carved too early, arranged on a platter and, in an hour or so after the cut surface is exposed to the air, the meat turns grey – so disappointing. However, a very easy solution is to carve the cold fillet up to 6 hours ahead and then reassemble it back into a roast fillet shape, wrapping it tightly in clingfilm. Then just arrange it on the platter immediately before serving. Ask the butcher to tie the joint neatly so that it keeps its round shape during roasting.

If you like very hot horseradish, use hot horseradish instead of the creamed. For me, life is too short to grate fresh horseradish!

1.6–1.8kg (3½–4 lb) fillet of beef, middle cut
12 large sprigs fresh thyme
3 garlic cloves, crushed
3 tablespoons olive oil
salt and freshly ground black pepper
fresh parsley, to garnish (optional)

HORSERADISH SAUCE
generous ½ x 185g jar horseradish cream
3 tablespoons whipped or thick cream

1 First marinate the beef. Put the fillet into a strong polythene bag with the thyme, garlic, oil, salt and pepper. Keep in the fridge in the marinade for up to 24 hours.

Preheat the oven to 220°C/Fan 200°C/Gas 7. Line a roasting tin with foil.

2 Heat a non-stick frying pan until hot. Lift the beef out of the marinade and drain. Set aside the thyme and pour the marinade into the hot frying pan to heat. When hot, seal the beef on all sides. When gloriously brown, lift out on to the prepared roasting tin and sprinkle with salt.
3 Roast in the preheated oven for a total of 25 minutes. If you have a meat thermometer, the internal temperature should be 60°C for rare; for not quite so rare, 62–63°C.

Serves 10 (or more depending upon whether you are serving other cold meats as well)

TO PREPARE AHEAD
Marinate the fillet for 24 hours, then cook it, cool quickly and put in the fridge, leaving it whole, up to 24 hours ahead. Take out of the fridge before carving. Carve the cold beef fillet up to 6 hours ahead, reassemble it back into a roast fillet shape, and wrap tightly in clingfilm. Arrange on the platter immediately before serving. Not suitable for freezing.

TO COOK IN THE AGA
In step 2, brown the marinated meat first on the Boiling Plate, then roast in the middle of the Roasting Oven for about 25 minutes.

4 Leave to become completely cold before carving (see introduction).

5 Mix together the horseradish cream and the cream.

6 For a nice garnish, fry the reserved fresh thyme, which makes it bright green, or just decorate with parsley. Serve the beef with the horseradish sauce.

Italian Tarragon Chicken

Serves 10

This is a perfect dish for a buffet, as it is easy and feeds a crowd. Serve with rice and a fresh leaf salad.

10 chicken breasts, skinned	3 large onions, sliced
salt and freshly ground black pepper	3 garlic cloves, crushed
	3 x 400g cans chopped tomatoes
2 small bunches fresh tarragon	50g (2 oz) plain flour
425ml (14 fl oz) chicken stock	150ml (5 fl oz) white wine
2 tablespoons olive oil	2 tablespoons redcurrant jelly

Preheat the oven to 200°C/Fan 180°C/Gas 6. You will need a roasting tin large enough to take the chicken breasts in a single layer.

1 Line the tin with a large sheet of foil with a wide overhang, enough to cover the top of the tin later.

2 Arrange the chicken in the prepared tin and season well. Chop the tarragon leaves and set aside; scatter the stalks over the chicken. Heat the stock to boiling and pour over the chicken. Bring the extra foil up over the chicken and crimp the edges to make a sealed tent.

3 Poach the chicken in the preheated oven for about 20 minutes, or until cooked through, but still pale. Set aside to cool in the stock. Measure out 250ml (9 fl oz) stock for use later.

4 Heat the oil in a large non-stick frying pan, add the onions and garlic, and fry for 1 minute. Lower the heat, cover and simmer for about 15 minutes, or until soft. Stir in the tomatoes, bring to the boil, and season well.

5 In a small bowl, blend together the flour and a little of the wine, and mix well. Pour in the remaining wine, stirring until smooth. Spoon a little of the hot tomato liquid into the flour and wine mixture, and mix until smooth. Pour into the pan with the onions and tomatoes, and bring to the boil, stirring continuously. Add redcurrant jelly to taste, and check the seasoning. As the sauce thickens, pour in the reserved 250ml (9 fl oz) poaching liquid, stirring constantly, to give a coating consistency.

6 Drain the chicken, cut into even-sized pieces, and add to the tomato sauce with the chopped tarragon. Fold in and serve hot.

TO PREPARE AHEAD

Make up to the end of step 6 about 24 hours ahead and reheat in a shallow ovenproof dish, covered with foil, at 200°C/Fan 180°C/Gas 6, for about 20 minutes, stirring from time to time until very hot. Take care not to overcook. This freezes well cooked, for up to 1 month.

TO COOK IN THE AGA

Poach the chicken in the Simmering Oven for about 40 minutes, or until tender. If you are in a hurry, cook in the Roasting Oven for 15 minutes. Soften the onion for the sauce, covered, in the Simmering Oven for about 15 minutes.

Serves 10

TO PREPARE AHEAD

Complete up to end of step 4 up to 24 hours ahead. It will freeze, but the mash may be a little on the wet side when thawed and cooked, so I usually freeze without the mash.

TO COOK IN THE AGA

Cook near to the top of the Roasting Oven for about 25–35 minutes, or until golden brown and piping hot.

Rather Special Cottage Pie with Horseradish Mash

This is a great recipe for a crowd. I've tried all kinds of potato toppings for this recipe, and for me the horseradish mash is the best. If you don't have a really large lasagne-type dish, use two smaller ones, and cook for a little less time.

2 tablespoons sunflower oil
1.5kg (3 lb 5 oz) raw minced beef
3 onions, roughly chopped
2 level tablespoons plain flour
425ml (14 fl oz) beef stock
150ml (5 fl oz) port
2 fat garlic cloves, crushed
225g (8 oz) chestnut mushrooms, sliced
6 tablespoons Worcestershire sauce
3 tablespoons tomato purée

salt and freshly ground black pepper

HORSERADISH MASH
1.5kg (3 lb 5 oz) King Edward potatoes, peeled
50g (2 oz) butter
¾ jar (about 120ml) creamed horseradish
a little milk
100g (4 oz) Cheddar, grated

Preheat the oven to 200°C/Fan 180°C/Gas 6. You will need a shallow ovenproof dish about 35 x 25 x 5cm (14 x 10 x 2 in).

1 Heat the oil in a large frying pan. Add the minced beef and brown over a high heat. Add the onions and fry until starting to soften. Sprinkle in the flour and stir to coat the meat and onions. Blend in some of the stock slowly at first, allowing it to thicken, then add the rest of the stock and all of the port. Bring to the boil, and stir in the garlic, mushrooms, Worcestershire sauce, tomato purée and some seasoning.
2 Cover with a lid and simmer gently for about 45 minutes, or until the mince is tender. Spoon into the ovenproof dish and leave to cool while making the mash topping.
3 Cut the peeled potatoes into chunks, put into a large saucepan, cover with water and add some salt. Bring to the boil and simmer until tender, about 20 minutes (depending on size). Drain the potatoes, add the

butter and mash until smooth. Beat in the creamed horseradish, adding more seasoning if necessary. Pour in a little milk, if needed, to make a spreading consistency.

4 Spread the mash over the cold mince. Decorate with the prongs of a fork and sprinkle over the cheese.

5 Cook in the preheated oven for about 30–35 minutes, or until the top is golden brown and the meat is hot in the middle.

Malaysian Rice

A great buffet recipe, or you can halve the quantity for fewer people. It's full of flavour, and easy to serve in a bowl with a fork.

Serves 10

450g (1 lb) easy-cook long-grain rice
salt and freshly ground black pepper
6 tablespoons olive oil
450g (1 lb) pork fillet, sliced into thin strips
2 tablespoons runny honey
12 rashers smoked streaky bacon, chopped

2 large onions, chopped
3 garlic cloves, crushed
1 tablespoon medium curry powder
¼ teaspoon chilli powder
8 tablespoons dark soy sauce
4 large spring onions, sliced
200g (7 oz) frozen petits pois
10 eggs

Preheat the oven to 200°C/Fan 180°C/Gas 6. Butter a large ovenproof dish.

1 Cook the rice in boiling salted water according to the packet instructions. Drain, refresh in cold water and set aside.
2 Heat 2 tablespoons of the oil in a large non-stick frying pan over a high heat. Add the pork and pour over the honey. Fry until golden brown, for about 3 minutes, turning the meat as it browns. Remove with a slotted spoon and set aside.
3 Heat a further 2 tablespoons oil in the pan, add the bacon and onions, and fry for 2–3 minutes. Lower the heat, cover and simmer for about 10 minutes, or until the bacon is cooked and the onions are soft.
4 Add the garlic and spices, and fry over a high heat for a moment. Add the rice, pork, soy sauce, spring onions and peas. Mix together and season with freshly ground black pepper.
5 Pour into the prepared dish and cook in the preheated oven, stirring occasionally, for about 30 minutes, or until the top is crisp and piping hot.
6 Meanwhile, heat the remaining oil in a large pan, and fry the eggs. Lift out carefully and drain on kitchen paper.
7 Serve the rice hot, topped with 1 fried egg per person.

TO PREPARE AHEAD
Make up to end of step 4 and turn into a serving dish. Cool, cover and keep in the fridge for up to 36 hours. Not suitable for freezing.

TO COOK IN THE AGA
At step 5, roast on the top set of runners in the Roasting Oven for about 25 minutes. Fry the eggs on the Boiling Plate.

Mary Berry's Stress-free Kitchen

Celebration Salmon en Croûte

This is a perfect recipe for numbers, and it looks so impressive too. Raw salmon is wrapped in spinach (you need large leaves) and assembled in a block like a Battenburg cake, held together with a salmon stuffing, then wrapped in puff pastry. When you trim the salmon, don't be afraid of trimming away a fair quantity because you need about 200g (7 oz) to make the stuffing. The Fresh Herb Dip on page 9, thinned down with a little single cream, would make a good sauce.

2 x 750g (1¾ lb) salmon
  fillets, skinned and tiny bones
  removed (pinboned)
1 egg white
1 small bunch fresh dill, chopped
100g (4 oz) capers, drained and
  roughly chopped

salt and freshly ground black
  pepper
20–25 very large spinach leaves
1 x 450g packet all-butter puff
  pastry
1 egg, beaten

1 Place the salmon fillets on a large chopping board and trim them into 2 neat symmetrical rectangles. Put the salmon trimmings into a processor with the egg white and dill, and whizz into a smooth paste. Remove the blade and stir in the capers and some seasoning. Set aside. Slice the salmon fillets in half lengthways so you have 4 even strips.

2 Take a spinach leaf and, holding it by the stalk, blanch in boiling water for 20 seconds until it has just wilted. Spread the leaf out on kitchen paper to dry while you repeat with the other leaves. Arrange about 4 or 5 large spinach leaves on the work surface so they are slightly overlapping. Put 1 strip of salmon on top, season well and roll up neatly and tightly in the leaves so the whole strip is covered in the spinach. Repeat with the remaining spinach and salmon strips, so that you have 4 spinach-encased strips.

3 Roll out the puff pastry thinly to a large rectangle about 50 x 40cm (20 x 16 in), or long enough to cover the salmon, and place on a large greased baking sheet. Put 2 salmon strips next to each other on one long side of the pastry about 10cm (4 in) from the edge. Spread the

Serves 10

TO PREPARE AHEAD
This can be made and cooked up to a day ahead, and reheated to serve. It also freezes well, uncooked, for up to 2 months.

TO COOK IN THE AGA
Bake on the floor of the Roasting Oven for 35–40 minutes, then rest on the top for about 15 minutes before serving.

salmon-trimming paste on top of the strips, Place the remaining 2 salmon strips on top, pressing them into the paste, creating a tight loaf. Brush the pastry around the outside of the fish with beaten egg, then fold over the pastry, pressing down to seal. Trim any pastry around the salmon leaving a 5cm (2 in) border. Crimp the edges using your fingers. Place in the fridge to firm up for 1 hour or so, or overnight.

Preheat the oven to 220°C/Fan 200°C/Gas 7.

4 Brush the pastry with the beaten egg and bake in the preheated oven for about 30–45 minutes, or until deep golden brown. Remove from the oven to rest for 15 minutes before serving.

Lamb Madras

This is perfect for a curry party for 10 people. There are quite a few ingredients, but it is worth it for an authentic, flavoursome curry. You will find curry leaves and tamarind paste sold in the spices or ethnic section. Serve with Creamy Vegetable Curry (see page 186) and warm naan bread, poppadums, mango chutney, Rice and Raita (see page 85).

4 tablespoons vegetable oil

1kg (2½ lb) diced leg of lamb

5 cm (2 in) piece fresh ginger root, peeled and sliced

4 garlic cloves

1 large green chilli

1 tablespoon each of ground cumin, ground coriander, garam masala and whole fenugreek seeds

2 large onions, cut into chunks

1 x 500g carton tomato passata

300ml (10 fl oz) chicken or beef stock

8 freeze-dried curry leaves, from a jar

1 cinnamon stick

3 tablespoons tomato purée

salt and freshly ground black pepper

2 tablespoons tamarind paste, from a jar

225g (8 oz) fresh baby spinach

Preheat the oven to 160°C/Fan 140°C/Gas 3.

1 Heat 2 tablespoons of the oil in a large non-stick pan or casserole dish. Brown the diced lamb on all sides (you may need to do this in batches). Remove with a slotted spoon and set aside.

2 Put the ginger, garlic and chilli into a small blender and whizz until roughly chopped. Heat a small pan and toast the ground spices and fenugreek seeds for 2–3 minutes, or until golden. Add the toasted spices to the blender and whizz again. If you don't have a small blender, pound with a pestle in a mortar.

3 Heat the remaining oil in the non-stick pan used for the lamb, add the onions and fry for 2–3 minutes. Stir in the spice paste and fry for 1 minute. Add the browned lamb, tomato passata, stock, curry leaves, cinnamon stick and tomato purée. Stir well, season and bring to the boil. Cover and transfer to the preheated oven for about 1 hour, or until the lamb is tender.

4 Add the tamarind paste and spinach, and heat over a high heat for about 3–4 minutes, or until the spinach has just wilted. Remove the cinnamon stick. Serve hot with warm naan bread.

Serves 10

TO PREPARE AHEAD

Make to the end of step 3 up to 2 days ahead and keep covered in the fridge. Reheat and continue with the recipe. Not suitable for freezing.

TO COOK IN THE AGA

At the end of step 3, cover and transfer to the Simmering Oven for about 1¼ hours, or until the lamb is tender.

Drinks

Parties can occur at any time of day, and just as you need different types of food, so you probably need different types of drinks. For a summer afternoon party in the garden, for instance, you could offer Iced Tea; for celebrations, hand round Elderflower 'Champagne'. For cocktails, mix up a Bellini, or for those coming hot and bothered off the tennis court or golf course, a refreshing Gunners. I've also included a Real Irish Coffee, which would make the perfect finish to a delicious dinner. Cheers!

Elderflower 'Champagne'

Although I call this classic elderflower recipe 'champagne', it is actually a non-alcoholic cordial. I have added Campden tablets, used in wine-making, to give it a longer life (both citric acid and Campden tablets can be bought from good pharmacies). Elderflower heads can be picked from the hedgerows from the end of May for about 1 month.

1.6kg (3½ lb) granulated sugar
1.4 litres (2½ pints) water
3 lemons
about 25 elderflower heads
50g (2 oz) citric acid
2 Campden tablets

TO SERVE
chilled sparkling water
ice cubes
lemon or lime slices
sprigs fresh mint

1 Measure the sugar and water into a large pan. Bring to the boil, stirring, until the sugar has dissolved. Remove from the heat and leave to cool.

2 Slice the lemons thinly by hand or in a processor. Put into a large plastic box or bucket.

3 Add the elderflower heads to the lemons. Stir in the citric acid and Campden tablets. Pour over the cooled sugar syrup. Cover and leave overnight or up to 2–3 days.

4 Sieve, then strain through muslin into bottles and store in the fridge (see below).

5 To serve, dilute to taste with chilled sparkling water and ice. If making in a jug, float some lemon or lime slices and fresh mint on the top.

Makes about 1.5 litres (2½ pints)

TO PREPARE AHEAD
The champagne base will keep for 2–3 months, but use up within 6 months. The elderflower heads can be frozen; freeze in bags of 25 heads. When using, put into the hot syrup straight from the freezer. Do not thaw first, or they will turn the syrup a sludgy brown colour.

Serves 4

Bellini

A peach version of Buck's Fizz, which is delicious! Whizzing up whole peaches in a processor makes it too bitty – it's much smoother with bought peach juice. This can also be made with sparkling white wine, but I prefer it with champagne.

100ml (4 fl oz) peach juice, from
  a bottle
300ml (10 fl oz) champagne

1 Mix the two ingredients together – it's as easy as that.

Serves 2

Gunners

This is one of my husband's favourite drinks. After every round of golf, he has this at the nineteenth tee! It really needs to be made and served straightaway, otherwise the ginger beer will lose its fizz.

600ml (1 pint) ginger beer
100ml (4 fl oz) lime cordial
2–3 drops of Angostura bitters
ice cubes, to serve

1 Pour the ginger beer and lime cordial into a small jug.
2 Add 2–3 drops of Angostura and stir well.
3 Put 2–3 ice cubes into 2 large glasses and pour over the drink. Serve immediately.

Real Irish Coffee

Serves 2

Delicious after a special meal or a long walk in a cold winter's day ... or think up your own excuse! It is very important to use pouring double cream, as single cream or thick cream would sink to the bottom of the glass. The sugar also helps to prevent the cream sinking. The coffee can, of course, be served without cream if preferred. For a change, replace the whiskey with Tia Maria or Grand Marnier.

4 teaspoons caster sugar
300ml (10 fl oz) good-quality,
  hot, strong black coffee

4 good tablespoons Irish whiskey
about 3 tablespoons pouring
  double cream, chilled

1 Warm a heatproof glass or small coffee cup with hot water. Pour out.
2 Add the sugar and a little of the hot coffee to each glass or cup, and stir to dissolve the sugar. Add the whiskey.
3 Pour in the remaining hot coffee, but not quite to the brim.
4 Gently pour the double cream on to the back of a teaspoon held over the coffee. The cream should float on the top.

Iced Tea

Serves 4–6 (makes 750ml/ 1¼ pints)

Very refreshing, especially on a hot summer's day. It is important to use bottled cold water as sometimes tap water can leave a scum that floats to the top. For variations, use Earl Grey, or some of the types of Indian or China teas.

3 ordinary tea bags
150ml (5 fl oz) boiling water
600ml (1 pint) bottled still water,
  cold

3 tablespoons caster sugar
ice cubes
slices of lemon to garnish
  (optional)

1 Put the tea bags into a large heatproof jug or bowl. Pour over the boiling water and leave to stand for about 5 minutes.
2 Remove the tea bags, pour in the cold water and add the sugar. Stir.
3 To serve, put an ice cube in a glass and pour over the tea. Garnish with lemon if liked.

Index